The War of the Classes

Jack London

Paperback ISBN: 1-57646-664-7

Quiet Vision Publishing
World Wide Web: http://www.quietvision.com

Printed and bound in the United States of America
Published - July 2003

Table of Contents

Preface

WHEN I was a youngster I was looked upon as a weird sort of creature, because, forsooth, I was a socialist. Reporters from local papers interviewed me, and the interviews, when published, were pathological studies of a strange and abnormal specimen of man. At that time (nine or ten years ago), because I made a stand in my native town for municipal ownership of public utilities, I was branded a "red-shirt," a "dynamiter," and an "anarchist"; and really decent fellows, who liked me very well, drew the line at my appearing in public with their sisters.

But the times changed. There came a day when I heard, in my native town, a Republican mayor publicly proclaim that "municipal ownership was a fixed American policy." And in that day I found myself picking up in the world. No longer did the pathologist study me, while the really decent fellows did not mind in the least the propinquity of myself and their sisters in the public eye. My political and sociological ideas were ascribed to the vagaries of youth, and good-natured elderly men patronized me and told me that I would grow up some day and become an unusually intelligent member of the community. Also they told me that my views were biassed by my empty pockets, and that some day, when I had gathered to me a few dollars, my views would be wholly different, — in short, that my views would be their views.

And then came the day when my socialism grew respectable, — still a vagary of youth, it was held, but romantically respectable. Romance, to the bourgeois mind, was respectable because it was not dangerous. As a "red-shirt," with bombs in all his pockets, I was dangerous. As a youth with nothing more menacing than a few philosophical ideas, Germanic in their origin, I was an interesting and pleasing personality.

Through all this experience I noted one thing. It was not I that changed, but the community. In fact, my socialistic views grew solider and more pronounced. I repeat, it was the community that changed, and to my chagrin I discovered that the community changed to such purpose that it was not above stealing my thunder. The community branded me a "red-shirt" because I stood for municipal ownership; a little later it applauded its mayor when he proclaimed municipal ownership to be a fixed American policy. He

1

The War of Classes

stole my thunder, and the community applauded the theft. And today the community is able to come around and give me points on municipal ownership.

What happened to me has been in no wise different from what has happened to the socialist movement as a whole in the United States. In the bourgeois mind socialism has changed from a terrible disease to a youthful vagary, and later on had its thunder stolen by the two old parties, — socialism, like a meek and thrifty workingman, being exploited became respectable.

Only dangerous things are abhorrent. The thing that is not dangerous is always respectable. And so with socialism in the United States. For several years it has been very respectable, — a sweet and beautiful Utopian dream, in the bourgeois mind, yet a dream, only a dream. During this period, which has just ended, socialism was tolerated because it was impossible and non-menacing. Much of its thunder had been stolen, and the workingmen had been made happy with full dinner-pails. There was nothing to fear. The kind old world spun on, coupons were clipped, and larger profits than ever were extracted from the toilers. Coupon-clipping and profit-extracting would continue to the end of time. These were functions divine in origin and held by divine right. The newspapers, the preachers, and the college presidents said so, and what they say, of course, is so — to the bourgeois mind.

Then came the presidential election of 1904. Like a bolt out of a clear sky was the socialist vote of 435,000, — an increase of nearly 400 per cent in four years, the largest third-party vote, with one exception, since the Civil War. Socialism had shown that it was a very live and growing revolutionary force, and all its old menace revived. I am afraid that neither it nor I are any longer respectable. The capitalist press of the country confirms me in my opinion, and herewith I give a few post-election utterances of the capitalist press: —

"The Democratic party of the constitution is dead. The Social-Democratic party of continental Europe, preaching discontent and class hatred, assailing law, property, and personal rights, and insinuating confiscation and plunder, is here." — Chicago Chronicle.

"That over forty thousand votes should have been cast in this city to make such a person as Eugene V. Debs the President of the United States is about the worst kind of

2

Preface

advertising that Chicago could receive." — Chicago Inter-Ocean.

"We cannot blink the fact that socialism is making rapid growth in this country, where, of all others, there would seem to be less inspiration for it." — Brooklyn Daily Eagle.

"Upon the hands of the Republican party an awful responsibility was placed last Tuesday. . . It knows that reforms — great, far-sweeping reforms — are necessary, and it has the power to make them. God help our civilization if it does not! . . . It must repress the trusts or stand before the world responsible for our system of government being changed into a social republic. The arbitrary cutting down of wages must cease, or socialism will seize another lever to lift itself into power." — The Chicago New World.

"Scarcely any phase of the election is more sinisterly interesting than the increase in the socialist vote. Before election we said that we could not afford to give aid and comfort to the socialists in any manner. . . It (socialism) must be fought in all its phases, in its every manifestation." — San Francisco Argonaut.

And far be it from me to deny that socialism is a menace. It is its purpose to wipe out, root and branch, all capitalistic institutions of present-day society. It is distinctly revolutionary, and in scope and depth is vastly more tremendous than any revolution that has ever occurred in the history of the world. It presents a new spectacle to the astonished world, — that of an *organized, international, revolutionary movement.* In the bourgeois mind a class struggle is a terrible and hateful thing, and yet that is precisely what socialism is, — a world-wide class struggle between the propertyless workers and the propertied masters of workers. It is the prime preachment of socialism that the struggle is a class struggle. The working class, in the process of social evolution, (in the very nature of things), is bound to revolt from the sway of the capitalist class and to overthrow the capitalist class. This is the menace of socialism, and in affirming it and in tallying myself an adherent of it, I accept my own consequent unrespectability.

As yet, to the average bourgeois mind, socialism is merely a menace, vague and formless. The average member of the capitalist class, when he discusses socialism, is condemned an ignoramus out

3

The War of Classes

of his own mouth. He does not know the literature of socialism, its philosophy, nor its politics. He wags his head sagely and rattles the dry bones of dead and buried ideas. His lips mumble mouldy phrases, such as, "Men are not born equal and never can be;" "It is Utopian and impossible;" "Abstinence should be rewarded;" "Man will first have to be born again;" "Cooperative colonies have always failed;" and "What if we do divide up? in ten years there would be rich and poor men such as there are today."

It surely is time that the capitalists knew something about this socialism that they feel menaces them. And it is the hope of the writer that the socialistic studies in this volume may in some slight degree enlighten a few capitalistic minds. The capitalist must learn, first and for always, that socialism is based, not upon the equality, but upon the inequality, of men. Next, he must learn that no new birth into spiritual purity is necessary before socialism becomes possible. He must learn that socialism deals with what is, not with what ought to be; and that the material with which it deals is the "clay of the common road," the warm human, fallible and frail, sordid and petty, absurd and contradictory, even grotesque, and yet, withal, shot through with flashes and glimmerings of something finer and God-like, with here and there sweetnesses of service and unselfishness, desires for goodness, for renunciation and sacrifice, and with conscience, stern and awful, at times blazingly imperious, demanding the right, — the right, nothing more nor less than the right.

Jack London.
Oakland, California.
January 12, 1905.

The Class Struggle

UNFORTUNATELY or otherwise, people are prone to believe in the reality of the things they think ought to be so. This comes of the cheery optimism which is innate with life itself; and, while it may sometimes be deplored, it must never be censured, for, as a rule, it is productive of more good than harm, and of about all the achievement there is in the world. There are cases where this optimism has been disastrous, as with the people who lived in Pompeii during its last quivering days; or with the aristocrats of the time of Louis XVI, who confidently expected the Deluge to overwhelm their children, or their children's children, but never themselves. But there is small likelihood that the case of perverse optimism here to be considered will end in such disaster, while there is every reason to believe that the great change now manifesting itself in society will be as peaceful and orderly in its culmination as it is in its present development.

Out of their constitutional optimism, and because a class struggle is an abhorred and dangerous thing, the great American people are unanimous in asserting that there is no class struggle. And by "American people" is meant the recognized and authoritative mouth-pieces of the American people, which are the press, the pulpit, and the university. The journalists, the preachers, and the professors are practically of one voice in declaring that there is no such thing as a class struggle now going on, much less that a class struggle will ever go on, in the United States. And this declaration they continually make in the face of a multitude of facts which impeach, not so much their sincerity, as affirm, rather, their optimism.

There are two ways of approaching the subject of the class struggle. The existence of this struggle can be shown theoretically, and it can be shown actually. For a class struggle to exist in society there must be, first, a class inequality, a superior class and an inferior class (as measured by power); and, second, the outlets must be closed whereby the strength and ferment of the inferior class have been permitted to escape.

That there are even classes in the United States is vigorously denied by many; but it is incontrovertible, when a group of individuals is formed, wherein the members are bound together by

5

The War of the Classes

common interests which are peculiarly their interests and not the interests of individuals outside the group, that such a group is a class. The owners of capital, with their dependents, form a class of this nature in the United States; the working people form a similar class. The interest of the capitalist class, say, in the matter of income tax, is quite contrary to the interest of the laboring class; and, *vice versa,* in the matter of poll-tax.

If between these two classes there be a clear and vital conflict of interest, all the factors are present which make a class struggle; but this struggle will lie dormant if the strong and capable members of the inferior class be permitted to leave that class and join the ranks of the superior class. The capitalist class and the working class have existed side by side and for a long time in the United States; but hitherto all the strong, energetic members of the working class have been able to rise out of their class and become owners of capital. They were enabled to do this because an undeveloped country with an expanding frontier gave equality of opportunity to all. In the almost lottery-like scramble for the ownership of vast unowned natural resources, and in the exploitation of which there was little or no competition of capital, (the capital itself rising out of the exploitation), the capable, intelligent member of the working class found a field in which to use his brains to his own advancement. Instead of being discontented in direct ratio with his intelligence and ambitions, and of radiating amongst his fellows a spirit of revolt as capable as he was capable, he left them to their fate and carved his own way to a place in the superior class.

But the day of an expanding frontier, of a lottery-like scramble for the ownership of natural resources, and of the upbuilding of new industries, is past. Farthest West has been reached, and an immense volume of surplus capital roams for investment and nips in the bud the patient efforts of the embryo capitalist to rise through slow increment from small beginnings. The gateway of opportunity after opportunity has been closed, and closed for all time. Rockefeller has shut the door on oil, the American Tobacco Company on tobacco, and Carnegie on steel. After Carnegie came Morgan, who triple-locked the door. These doors will not open again, and before them pause thousands of ambitious young men to read the placard: *No Thorough-Fare*

And day by day more doors are shut, while the ambitious young men continue to be born. It is they, denied the opportunity to rise from the working class, who preach revolt to the working class.

The Class Struggle

Had he been born fifty years later, Andrew Carnegie, the poor Scotch boy, might have risen to be president of his union, or of a federation of unions; but that he would never have become the builder of Homestead and the founder of multitudinous libraries, is as certain as it is certain that some other man would have developed the steel industry had Andrew Carnegie never been born.

Theoretically, then, there exist in the United States all the factors which go to make a class struggle. There are the capitalists and working classes, the interests of which conflict, while the working class is no longer being emasculated to the extent it was in the past by having drawn off from it its best blood and brains. Its more capable members are no longer able to rise out of it and leave the great mass leaderless and helpless. They remain to be its leaders.

But the optimistic mouthpieces of the great American people, who are themselves deft theoreticians, are not to be convinced by mere theoretics. So it remains to demonstrate the existence of the class struggle by a marshalling of the facts.

When nearly two millions of men, finding themselves knit together by certain interests peculiarly their own, band together in a strong organization for the aggressive pursuit of those interests, it is evident that society has within it a hostile and warring class. But when the interests which this class aggressively pursues conflict sharply and vitally with the interests of another class, class antagonism arises and a class struggle is the inevitable result. One great organization of labor alone has a membership of 1,700,000 in the United States. This is the American Federation of Labor, and outside of it are many other large organizations. All these men are banded together for the frank purpose of bettering their condition, regardless of the harm worked thereby upon all other classes. They are in open antagonism with the capitalist class, while the manifestos of their leaders state that the struggle is one which can never end until the capitalist class is exterminated.

Their leaders will largely deny this last statement, but an examination of their utterances, their actions, and the situation will forestall such denial. In the first place, the conflict between labor and capital is over the division of the join product. Capital and labor apply themselves to raw material and make it into a finished product. The difference between the value of the raw material and the value of the finished product is the value they have added to it by their joint effort. This added value is, therefore, their joint product, and it is over the division of this joint product that the struggle between labor and capital takes place. Labor takes its share in wages; capital takes its share in profits. It is patent, if capital took in profits the whole joint product, that labor would perish. And it is equally patent, if labor took in wages the whole joint product, that capital would perish. Yet this last is the very thing labor aspires to do, and that it will never be content with anything less than the whole joint product is evidenced by the words of its leaders.

Mr. Samuel Gompers, president of the American Federation of Labor, has said: "The workers want more wages; more of the comforts of life; more leisure; more chance for self-improvement as men, as trade-unionists, as citizens. *These were the wants of yesterday; they are the wants of today; they will be the wants of tomorrow, and of tomorrow's morrow.* The struggle may assume new forms, but the issue is the immemorial one, — an effort of the producers to obtain an increasing measure of the wealth that flows from their production."

Mr. Henry White, secretary of the United Garment Workers of America and a member of the Industrial Committee of the National Civic Federation, speaking of the National Civic Federation soon after its inception, said: "To fall into one another's arms, to avow friendship, to express regret at the injury which has been done, would not alter the facts of the situation. Workingmen will continue to demand more pay, and the employer will naturally oppose them. The readiness and ability of the workmen to fight will, as usual, largely determine the amount of their wages or their share in the product. . . But when it comes to dividing the proceeds, there is the rub. We can also agree that the larger the product through the employment of labor-saving methods the better, as there will be more to be divided, but again the question of the division. . . . A Conciliation Committee, having the confidence of the community, and composed of men possessing practical knowledge of industrial affairs, can therefore aid in mitigating this antagonism, in preventing avoidable conflicts, in bringing about a *truce;* I use the word 'truce' because understandings can only be temporary."

Here is a man who might have owned cattle on a thousand hills, been a lumber baron or a railroad king, had he been born a few years sooner. As it is, he remains in his class, is secretary of the United Garment Workers of America, and is so thoroughly saturated with the class struggle that he speaks of the dispute between capital and labor in terms of war, — workmen *fight* with employ-

The Class Struggle

ers; it is possible to avoid some *conflicts;* in certain cases *truces* may be, for the time being, effected.

Man being man and a great deal short of the angels, the quarrel over the division of the joint product is irreconcilable. For the last twenty years in the United States, there has been an average of over a thousand strikes per year; and year by year these strikes increase in magnitude, and the front of the labor army grows more imposing. And it is a class struggle, pure and simple. Labor as a class is fighting with capital as a class.

Workingmen will continue to demand more pay, and employers will continue to oppose them. This is the key-note to *laissez faire,* — everybody for himself and devil take the hindmost. It is upon this that the rampant individualist bases his individualism. It is the let-alone policy, the struggle for existence, which strengthens the strong, destroys the weak, and makes a finer and more capable breed of men. But the individual has passed away and the group has come, for better or worse, and the struggle has become, not a struggle between individuals, but a struggle between groups. So the query rises: Has the individualist never speculated upon the labor group becoming strong enough to destroy the capitalist group, and take to itself and run for itself the machinery of industry? And, further, has the individualist never speculated upon this being still a triumphant expression of individualism, — of group individualism, — if the confusion of terms may be permitted?

But the facts of the class struggle are deeper and more significant than have so far been presented. A million or so of workmen may organize for the pursuit of interests which engender class antagonism and strife, and at the same time be unconscious of what is engendered. But when a million or so of workmen show unmistakable signs of being conscious of their class, — of being, in short, class conscious, — then the situation grows serious. The uncompromising and terrible hatred of the trade-unionist for a scab is the hatred of a class for a traitor to that class, — while the hatred of a trade-unionist for the militia is the hatred of a class for a weapon wielded by the class with which it is fighting. No workman can be true to his class and at the same time be a member of the militia: this is the dictum of the labor leaders.

In the town of the writer, the good citizens, when they get up a Fourth of July parade and invite the labor unions to participate, are informed by the unions that they will not march in the parade if the militia marches. Article 8 of the constitution of the Painters' and

The War of the Classes

Decorators' Union of Schenectady provides that a member must not be a "militiaman, special police officer, or deputy marshal in the employ of corporations or individuals during strikes, lockouts, or other labor difficulties, and any member occupying any of the above positions will be debarred from membership." Mr. William Potter was a member of this union and a member of the National Guard. As a result, because he obeyed the order of the Governor when his company was ordered out to suppress rioting, he was expelled from his union. Also his union demanded his employers, Shafer & Barry, to discharge him from their service. This they complied with, rather than face the threatened strike.

Mr. Robert L. Walker, first lieutenant of the Light Guards, a New Haven militia company, recently resigned. His reason was, that he was a member of the Car Builders' Union, and that the two organizations were antagonistic to each other. During a New Orleans street-car strike not long ago, a whole company of militia, called out to protect non-union men, resigned in a body. Mr. John Mulholland, president of the International Association of Allied Metal Mechanics, has stated that he does not want the members to join the militia. The Local Trades' Assembly of Syracuse, New York, has passed a resolution, by unanimous vote, requiring union men who are members of the National Guard to resign, under pain of expulsion, from the unions. The Amalgamated Sheet Metal Workers' Association has incorporated in its constitution an amendment excluding from membership in its organization "any person a member of the regular army, or of the State militia or naval reserve." The Illinois State Federation of Labor, at a recent convention, passed without a dissenting vote a resolution declaring that membership in military organizations is a violation of labor union obligations, and requesting all union men to withdraw from the militia. The president of the Federation, Mr. Albert Young, declared that the militia was a menace not only to unions, but to all workers throughout the country.

These instances may be multiplied a thousand fold. The union workmen are becoming conscious of their class, and of the struggle their class is waging with the capitalist class. To be a member of the militia is to be a traitor to the union, for the militia is a weapon wielded by the employers to crush the workers in the struggle between the warring groups.

Another interesting, and even more pregnant, phase of the class struggle is the political aspect of it as displayed by the socialists.

The Class Struggle

Five men, standing together, may perform prodigies; 500 men, marching as marched the historic Five Hundred of Marseilles, may sack a palace and destroy a king; while 500,000 men, passionately preaching the propaganda of a class struggle, waging a class struggle along political lines, and backed by the moral and intellectual support of 10,000,000 more men of like convictions throughout the world, may come pretty close to realizing a class struggle in these United States of ours.

In 1900 these men cast 150,000 votes; two years later, in 1902, they cast 300,000 votes; and in 1904 they cast 450,000. They have behind them a most imposing philosophic and scientific literature; they own illustrated magazines and reviews, high in quality, dignity, and restraint; they possess countless daily and weekly papers which circulate throughout the land, and single papers which have subscribers by the hundreds of thousands; and they literally swamp the working classes in a vast sea of tracts and pamphlets. No political party in the United States, no church organization nor mission effort, has as indefatigable workers as has the socialist party. They multiply themselves, know of no effort nor sacrifice too great to make for the Cause; and "Cause," with them, is spelled out in capitals. They work for it with a religious zeal, and would die for it with a willingness similar to that of the Christian martyrs.

These men are preaching an uncompromising and deadly class struggle. In fact, they are organized upon the basis of a class struggle. "The history of society," they say, "is a history of class struggles. Patrician struggled with plebeian in early Rome; the king and the burghers, with the nobles in the Middle Ages; later on, the king and the nobles with the bourgeoisie; and today the struggle is on between the triumphant bourgeoisie and the rising proletariat. By 'proletariat' is meant the class of people without capital which sells its labor for a living.

"That the proletariat shall conquer," (mark the note of fatalism), "is as certain as the rising sun. Just as the bourgeoisie of the eighteenth century wanted democracy applied to politics, so the proletariat of the twentieth century wants democracy applied to industry. As the bourgeoisie complained against the government being run by and for the nobles, so the proletariat complains against the government and industry being run by and for the bourgeoisie; and so, following in the footsteps of its predecessor, the proletariat will possess itself of the government, apply democracy to industry, abolish wages, which are merely legalized robbery, and run the

The War of the Classes

business of the country in its own interest."

"Their aim," they say, "is to organize the working class, and those in sympathy with it, into a political party, with the object of conquering the powers of government and of using them for the purpose of transforming the present system of private ownership of the means of production and distribution into collective ownership by the entire people."

Briefly stated, this is the battle plan of these 450,000 men who call themselves "socialists." And, in the face of the existence of such an aggressive group of men, a class struggle cannot very well be denied by the optimistic Americans who say: "A class struggle is monstrous. Sir, there is no class struggle." The class struggle is here, and the optimistic American had better gird himself for the fray and put a stop to it, rather than sit idly declaiming that what ought not to be is not, and never will be.

But the socialists, fanatics and dreamers though they may well be, betray a foresight and insight, and a genius for organization, which put to shame the class with which they are openly at war. Failing of rapid success in waging a sheer political propaganda, and finding that they were alienating the most intelligent and most easily organized portion of the voters, the socialists lessoned from the experience and turned their energies upon the trade-union movement. To win the trade unions was well-nigh to win the war, and recent events show that they have done far more winning in this direction than have the capitalists.

Instead of antagonizing the unions, which had been their previous policy, the socialists proceeded to conciliate the unions. "Let every good socialist join the union of his trade," the edict went forth. "Bore from within and capture the trade-union movement." And this policy, only several years old, has reaped fruits far beyond their fondest expectations. Today the great labor unions are honeycombed with socialists, "boring from within," as they picturesquely term their undermining labor. At work and at play, at business meeting and council, their insidious propaganda goes on. At the shoulder of the trade-unionist is the socialist, sympathizing with him, aiding him with head and hand, suggesting — perpetually suggesting — the necessity for political action. As the *Journal,* of Lansing, Michigan, a republican paper, has remarked: "The socialists in the labor unions are tireless workers. They are sincere, energetic, and self-sacrificing. . . . They stick to the union and work all the while, thus making a showing which, reckoned by ordinary standards, is out of all proportion to their numbers. Their cause is growing among union laborers, and their long fight, intended to turn the Federation into a political organization, is likely to win."

They miss no opportunity of driving home the necessity for political action, the necessity for capturing the political machinery of society whereby they may master society. As an instance of this is the avidity with which the American socialists seized upon the famous Taft-Vale Decision in England, which was to the effect that an unincorporated union could be sued and its treasury rifled by process of law. Throughout the United States, the socialists pointed the moral in similar fashion to the way it was pointed by the Social-Democratic Herald, which advised the trade-unionists, in view of the decision, to stop trying to fight capital with money, which they lacked, and to begin fighting with the ballot, which was their strongest weapon.

Night and day, tireless and unrelenting, they labor at their self-imposed task of undermining society. Mr. M. G. Cunniff, who lately made an intimate study of trade-unionism, says: "All through the unions socialism filters. Almost every other man is a socialist, preaching that unionism is but a makeshift." "Malthus be damned," they told him, "for the good time was coming when every man should be able to rear his family in comfort." In one union, with two thousand members, Mr. Cunniff found every man a socialist, and from his experiences Mr. Cunniff was forced to confess, "I lived in a world that showed our industrial life a-tremble from beneath with a never-ceasing ferment."

The socialists have already captured the Western Federation of Miners, the Western Hotel and Restaurant Employees' Union, and the Patternmakers' National Association. The Western Federation of Miners, at a recent convention, declared: "The strike has failed to secure to the working classes their liberty; we therefore call upon the workers to strike as one man for their liberties at the ballot box.... We put ourselves on record as committed to the programme of independent political action. . . . We indorse the platform of the socialist party, and accept it as the declaration of principles of our organization. We call upon our members as individuals to commence immediately the organization of the socialist movement in their respective towns and states, and to cooperate in every way for the furtherance of the principles of socialism and of the socialist party. In states where the socialist party has not perfected its organization, we advise that every assistance be given by our members to that end. . . . We therefore call for organizers, capable and well-versed in the whole programme of the labor movement, to be sent into each state to preach the necessity of organization on the political as well as on the economic field."

The capitalist class has a glimmering consciousness of the class struggle which is shaping itself in the midst of society; but the capitalists, as a class, seem to lack the ability for organizing, for coming together, such as is possessed by the working class. No American capitalist ever aids an English capitalist in the common fight, while workmen have formed international unions, the socialists a world-wide international organization, and on all sides space and race are bridged in the effort to achieve solidarity. Resolutions of sympathy, and, fully as important, donations of money, pass back and forth across the sea to wherever labor is fighting its pitched battles.

For divers reasons, the capitalist class lacks this cohesion or solidarity, chief among which is the optimism bred of past success. And, again, the capitalist class is divided; it has within itself a class struggle of no mean proportions, which tends to irritate and harass it and to confuse the situation. The small capitalist and the large capitalist are grappled with each other, struggling over what Achille Loria calls the "bi-partition of the revenues." Such a struggle, though not precisely analogous, was waged between the landlords and manufacturers of England when the one brought about the passage of the Factory Acts and the other the abolition of the Corn Laws.

Here and there, however, certain members of the capitalist class see clearly the cleavage in society along which the struggle is beginning to show itself, while the press and magazines are beginning to raise an occasional and troubled voice. Two leagues of class-conscious capitalists have been formed for the purpose of carrying on their side of the struggle. Like the socialists, they do not mince matters, but state boldly and plainly that they are fighting to subjugate the opposing class. It is the barons against the commons. One of these leagues, the National Association of Manufacturers, is stopping short of nothing in what it conceives to be a life-and-death struggle. Mr. D. M. Parry, who is the president of the league, as well as president of the National Metal Trades' Association, is leaving no stone unturned in what he feels to be a desperate effort to organize his class. He has issued the call to arms in terms every-

The Class Struggle

thing but ambiguous: *"There is still time in the United States to head off the socialistic programme, which, unrestrained, is sure to wreck our country."*

As he says, the work is for "federating employers in order that we may meet with a united front all issues that affect us. We must come to this sooner or later. . . . The work immediately before the National Association of Manufacturers is, first, *keep the vicious Eight-Hour Bill off the books;* second, to *destroy the Anti-Injunction Bill* which wrests your business from you and places it in the hands of your employees; third, to secure the *passage of the Department of Commerce and Industry Bill;* the latter would go through with a rush were it not for the hectoring opposition of Organized Labor." By this department, he further says, "business interests would have direct and sympathetic representation at Washington."

In a later letter, issued broadcast to the capitalists outside the League, President Parry points out the success which is already beginning to attend the efforts of the League at Washington. "We have contributed more than any other influence to the quick passage of the new Department of Commerce Bill. It is said that the activities of this office are numerous and satisfactory; but of that I must not say too much — or anything. . . . At Washington the Association is not represented too much, either directly or indirectly. Sometimes it is known in a most powerful way that it is represented vigorously and unitedly. Sometimes it is not known that it is represented at all."

The second class-conscious capitalist organization is called the National Economic League. It likewise manifests the frankness of men who do not dilly-dally with terms, but who say what they mean, and who mean to settle down to a long, hard fight. Their letter of invitation to prospective members opens boldly. "We beg to inform you that the National Economic League will render its services in an impartial educational movement *to oppose socialism and class hatred."* Among its class-conscious members, men who recognize that the opening guns of the class struggle have been fired, may be instanced the following names: Hon. Lyman J. Gage, Ex-Secretary U. S. Treasury; Hon. Thomas Jefferson Coolidge, Ex-Minister to France; Rev. Henry C. Potter, Bishop New York Diocese; Hon. John D. Long, Ex-Secretary U. S. Navy; Hon. Levi P. Morton, Ex-Vice President United States; Henry Clews; John F. Dryden, President Prudential Life Insurance Co.; John A. McCall, President New York Life Insurance Co.; J. L. Greatsinger, President

The War of the Classes

Brooklyn Rapid Transit Co.; the shipbuilding firm of William Cramp & Sons, the Southern Railway system, and the Atchison, Topeka, & Santa Fe Railway Company. Instances of the troubled editorial voice have not been rare during the last several years. There were many cries from the press during the last days of the anthracite coal strike that the mine owners, by their stubbornness, were sowing the regrettable seeds of socialism. The World's Work for December, 1902, said: "The next significant fact is the recommendation by the Illinois State Federation of Labor that all members of labor unions who are also members of the state militia shall resign from the militia. This proposition has been favorably regarded by some other labor organizations. It has done more than any other single recent declaration or action to cause a public distrust of such unions as favor it. *It hints of a classo separation that in turn hints of anarchy.*"

The *outlook,* February 14, 1903, in reference to the rioting at Waterbury, remarks, "That all this disorder should have occurred in a city of the character and intelligence of Waterbury indicates that the industrial war spirit is by no means confined to the immigrant or ignorant working classes."

That President Roosevelt has smelt the smoke from the firing line of the class struggle is evidenced by his words, "Above all we need to remember that any kind of *class animosity in the political world* is, if possible, even more destructive to national welfare than sectional, race, or religious animosity." The chief thing to be noted here is President Roosevelt's tacit recognition of class animosity in the industrial world, and his fear, which language cannot portray stronger, that this class animosity may spread to the political world. Yet this is the very policy which the socialists have announced in their declaration of war against present-day society — to capture the political machinery of society and by that machinery destroy present-day society.

The New York Independent for February 12, 1903, recognized without qualification the class struggle. "It is impossible fairly to pass upon the methods of labor unions, or to devise plans for remedying their abuses, until it is recognized, to begin with, that unions are based upon class antagonism and that their policies are dictated by the necessities of social warfare. A strike is a rebellion against the owners of property. The rights of property are protected by government. And a strike, under certain provocation, may extend as far as did the general strike in Belgium a few years since, when practically the entire wage-earning population stopped work in order to force political concessions from the property-owning classes. This is an extreme case, but it brings out vividly the real nature of labor organization as a species of warfare whose object is the coercion of one class by another class."

It has been shown, theoretically and actually, that there is a class struggle in the United States. The quarrel over the division of the joint product is irreconcilable. The working class is no longer losing its strongest and most capable members. These men, denied room for their ambition in the capitalist ranks, remain to be the leaders of the workers, to spur them to discontent, to make them conscious of their class, to lead them to revolt.

This revolt, appearing spontaneously all over the industrial field in the form of demands for an increased share of the joint product, is being carefully and shrewdly shaped for a political assault upon society. The leaders, with the carelessness of fatalists, do not hesitate for an instant to publish their intentions to the world. They intend to direct the labor revolt to the capture of the political machinery of society. With the political machinery once in their hands, which will also give them the control of the police, the army, the navy, and the courts, they will confiscate, with or without remuneration, all the possessions of the capitalist class which are used in the production and distribution of the necessaries and luxuries of life. By this, they mean to apply the law of eminent domain to the land, and to extend the law of eminent domain till it embraces the mines, the factories, the railroads, and the ocean carriers. In short, they intend to destroy present-day society, which they contend is run in the interest of another class, and from the materials to construct a new society, which will be run in their interest.

On the other hand, the capitalist class is beginning to grow conscious of itself and of the struggle which is being waged. It is already forming offensive and defensive leagues, while some of the most prominent figures in the nation are preparing to lead it in the attack upon socialism.

The question to be solved is not one of Malthusianism, "projected efficiency," nor ethics. It is a question of might. Whichever class is to win, will win by virtue of superior strength; for the workers are beginning to say, as they said to Mr. Cunniff, "Malthus be damned." In their own minds they find no sanction for continuing the individual struggle for the survival of the fittest. As Mr. Gompers has said, they want more, and more, and more.

The War of the Classes

The ethical import of Mr. Kidd's plan of the present generation putting up with less in order that race efficiency may be projected into a remote future, has no bearing upon their actions. They refuse to be the "glad perishers" so glowingly described by Nietzsche.

It remains to be seen how promptly the capitalist class will respond to the call to arms. Upon its promptness rests its existence, for if it sits idly by, soothfully proclaiming that what ought not to be cannot be, it will find the roof beams crashing about its head. The capitalist class is in the numerical minority, and bids fair to be outvoted if it does not put a stop to the vast propaganda being waged by its enemy. It is no longer a question of whether or not there is a class struggle. The question now is, what will be the outcome of the class struggle?

The Tramp

MR. FRANCIS O'NEIL, General Superintendent of Police, Chicago, speaking of the tramp, says: "Despite the most stringent police regulations, a great city will have a certain number of homeless vagrants to shelter through the winter." "Despite," — mark the word, a confession of organized helplessness as against unorganized necessity. If police regulations are stringent and yet fail, then that which makes them fail, namely, the tramp, must have still more stringent reasons for succeeding. This being so, it should be of interest to inquire into these reasons, to attempt to discover why the nameless and homeless vagrant sets at naught the right arm of the corporate power of our great cities, why all that is weak and worthless is stronger than all that is strong and of value.

Mr. O'Neil is a man of wide experience on the subject of tramps. He may be called a specialist. As he says of himself: "As an old-time desk sergeant and police captain, I have had almost unlimited opportunity to study and analyze this class of floating population, which seeks the city in winter and scatters abroad through the country in the spring." He then continues: "This experience reiterated the lesson that the vast majority of these wanderers are of the class with whom a life of vagrancy is a chosen means of living without work." Not only is it to be inferred from this that there is a large class in society which lives without work, for Mr. O'Neil's testimony further shows that this class is forced to live without work.

He says: "I have been astonished at the multitude of those who have unfortunately engaged in occupations which practically force them to become loafers for at least a third of the year. And it is from this class that the tramps are largely recruited. I recall a certain winter when it seemed to me that a large portion of the inhabitants of Chicago belonged to this army of unfortunates. I was stationed at a police station not far from where an ice harvest was ready for the cutters. The ice company advertised for helpers, and the very night this call appeared in the newspapers our station was packed with homeless men, who asked shelter in order to be at hand for the morning's work. Every foot of floor space was given over to these lodgers and scores were still unaccommodated."

And again: "And it must be confessed that the man who is

The War of the Classes

willing to do honest labor for food and shelter is a rare specimen in this vast army of shabby and tattered wanderers who seek the warmth of the city with the coming of the first snow." Taking into consideration the crowd of honest laborers that swamped Mr. O'Neil's station-house on the way to the ice-cutting, it is patent, if all tramps were looking for honest labor instead of a small minority, that the honest laborers would have a far harder task finding something honest to do for food and shelter. If the opinion of the honest laborers who swamped Mr. O'Neil's station-house were asked, one could rest confident that each and every man would express a preference for fewer honest laborers on the morrow when he asked the ice foreman for a job.

And, finally, Mr. O'Neil says: "The humane and generous treatment which this city has accorded the great army of homeless unfortunates has made it the victim of wholesale imposition, and this well-intended policy of kindness has resulted in making Chicago the winter Mecca of a vast and undesirable floating population." That is to say, because of her kindness, Chicago had more than her fair share of tramps; because she was humane and generous she suffered whole-sale imposition. From this we must conclude that it does not do to be *humane* and *generous* to our fellow-men — when they are tramps. Mr. O'Neil is right, and that this is no sophism it is the intention of this article, among other things, to show.

In a general way we may draw the following inferences from the remarks of Mr. O'Neil: (1) The tramp is stronger than organized society and cannot be put down; (2) The tramp is "shabby," "tattered," "homeless," "unfortunate"; (3) There is a "vast" number of tramps; (4) Very few tramps are willing to do honest work; (5) Those tramps who are willing to do honest work have to hunt very hard to find it; (6) The tramp is undesirable.

To this last let the contention be appended that the tramp is only *personally* undesirable; that he is *negatively* desirable; that the function he performs in society is a negative function; and that he is the by-product of economic necessity.

It is very easy to demonstrate that there are more men than there is work for men to do. For instance, what would happen tomorrow if one hundred thousand tramps should become suddenly inspired with an overmastering desire for work? It is a fair question. "Go to work" is preached to the tramp every day of his life. The judge on the bench, the pedestrian in the street, the housewife at the kitchen

The Tramp

door, all unite in advising him to go to work. So what would happen tomorrow if one hundred thousand tramps acted upon this advice and strenuously and indomitably sought work? Why, by the end of the week one hundred thousand workers, their places taken by the tramps, would receive their time and be "hitting the road" for a job.

Ella Wheeler Wilcox unwittingly and uncomfortably demonstrated the disparity between men and work.* She made a casual reference, in a newspaper column she conducts, to the difficulty two business men found in obtaining good employees. The first morning mail brought her seventy-five applications for the position, and at the end of two weeks over two hundred people had applied.

Still more strikingly was the same proposition recently demonstrated in San Francisco. A sympathetic strike called out a whole federation of trades' unions. Thousands of men, in many branches of trade, quit work, — draymen, sand teamsters, porters and packers, longshoremen, stevedores, warehousemen, stationary engineers, sailors, marine firemen, stewards, sea-cooks, and so forth, — an interminable list. It was a strike of large proportions. Every Pacific coast shipping city was involved, and the entire coasting service, from San Diego to Puget Sound, was virtually tied up. The time was considered auspicious. The Philippines and Alaska had drained the Pacific coast of surplus labor. It was summer-time, when the agricultural demand for laborers was at its height, and when the cities were bare of their floating populations. And yet there remained a body of surplus labor sufficient to take the places of the strikers. No matter what occupation, sea-cook or stationary engineer, sand teamster or warehouseman, in every case there was an idle worker ready to do the work. And not only ready but anxious. They fought for a chance to work. Men were killed, hundreds of heads were broken, the hospitals were filled with injured men, and thousands of assaults were committed. And still surplus laborers, "scabs," came forward to replace the strikers.

The question arises: *Whence came this second army of workers to replace the first army?* One thing is certain: the trades' unions did not scab on one another. Another thing is certain: no industry on the Pacific slope was crippled in the slightest degree by its workers being drawn away to fill the places of the strikers. A third

*"From 43 to 52 per cent of all applicants need work rather than relief." — Report of the Charity Organization Society of New York City.

The War of the Classes

thing is certain: the agricultural workers did not flock to the cities to replace the strikers. In this last instance it is worth while to note that the agricultural laborers wailed to High Heaven when a few of the strikers went into the country to compete with them in unskilled employments. So there is no accounting for this second army of workers. It simply was. It was there all this time, a surplus labor army in the year of our Lord 1901, a year adjudged most prosperous in the annals of the United States.*

The existence of the surplus labor army being established, there remains to be established the economic necessity for the surplus labor army. The simplest and most obvious need is that brought about by the fluctuation of production. If, when production is at low ebb, all men are at work, it necessarily follows that when production increases there will be no men to do the increased work. This may seem almost childish, and, if not childish, at least easily remedied. At low ebb let the men work shorter time; at high flood let them work overtime. The main objection to this is, that it is not done, and that we are considering what is, not what might be or should be.

Then there are great irregular and periodical demands for labor which must be met. Under the first head come all the big building and engineering enterprises. When a canal is to be dug or a railroad put through, requiring thousands of laborers, it would be hurtful to withdraw these laborers from the constant industries. And whether it is a canal to be dug or a cellar, whether five thousand men are required or five, it is well, in society as at present organized, that they be taken from the surplus labor army. The surplus labor army is the reserve fund of social energy, and this is one of the reasons for its existence.

Under the second head, periodical demands, come the harvests. Throughout the year, huge labor tides sweep back and forth across the United States. That which is sown and tended by few men, comes to sudden ripeness and must be gathered by many men; and it is inevitable that these many men form floating populations. In the late spring the berries must be picked, in the summer the grain garnered, in the fall, the hops gathered, in the winter the ice harvested. In California a man may pick berries in Siskiyou, peaches

*Mr. Leiter, who owns a coal mine at the town of Zeigler, Illinois, in an interview printed in the Chicago Record-Herald of December 6, 1904, said: "When I go into the market to purchase labor, I propose to retain just as much freedom as does a purchaser in any other kind of a market. . . . There is no difficulty whatever in obtaining labor, *for the country is full of unemployed men.*"

The Tramp

in Santa Clara, grapes in the San Joaquin, and oranges in Los Angeles, going from job to job as the season advances, and travelling a thousand miles ere the season is done. But the great demand for agricultural labor is in the summer. In the winter, work is slack, and these floating populations eddy into the cities to eke out a precarious existence and harrow the souls of the police officers until the return of warm weather and work. If there were constant work at good wages for every man, who would harvest the crops?

But the last and most significant need for the surplus labor army remains to be stated. This surplus labor acts as a check upon all employed labor. It is the lash by which the masters hold the workers to their tasks, or drive them back to their tasks when they have revolted. It is the goad which forces the workers into the compulsory "free contracts" against which they now and again rebel. There is only one reason under the sun that strikes fail, and that is because there are always plenty of men to take the strikers' places.

The strength of the union today, other things remaining equal, is proportionate to the skill of the trade, or, in other words, proportionate to the pressure the surplus labor army can put upon it. If a thousand ditch-diggers strike, it is easy to replace them, wherefore the ditch-diggers have little or no organized strength. But a thousand highly skilled machinists are somewhat harder to replace, and in consequence the machinist unions are strong. The ditch-diggers are wholly at the mercy of the surplus labor army, the machinists only partly. To be invincible, a union must be a monopoly. It must control every man in its particular trade, and regulate apprentices so that the supply of skilled workmen may remain constant; this is the dream of the "Labor Trust" on the part of the captains of labor.

Once, in England, after the Great Plague, labor awoke to find there was more work for men than there were men to work. Instead of workers competing for favors from employers, employers were competing for favors from the workers. Wages went up and up, and continued to go up, until the workers demanded the full product of their toil. Now it is clear that, when labor receives its full product capital must perish. And so the pygmy capitalists of that post-Plague day found their existence threatened by this untoward condition of affairs. To save themselves, they set a maximum wage, restrained the workers from moving about from place to place, smashed incipient organization, refused to tolerate idlers, and

The War of the Classes

by most barbarous legal penalties punished those who disobeyed. After that, things went on as before.

The point of this, of course, is to demonstrate the need of the surplus labor army. Without such an army, our present capitalist society would be powerless. Labor would organize as it never organized before, and the last least worker would be gathered into the unions. The full product of toil would be demanded, and capitalist society would crumble away. Nor could capitalist society save itself as did the post-Plague capitalist society. The time is past when a handful of masters, by imprisonment and barbarous punishment, can drive the legions of the workers to their tasks. Without a surplus labor army, the courts, police, and military are impotent. In such matters the function of the courts, police, and military is to preserve order, and to fill the places of strikers with surplus labor. If there be no surplus labor to instate, there is no function to perform; for disorder arises only during the process of instatement, when the striking labor army and the surplus labor army clash together. That is to say, that which maintains the integrity of the present industrial society more potently than the courts, police, and military is the surplus labor army.

It has been shown that there are more men than there is work for men, and that the surplus labor army is an economic necessity. To show how the tramp is a by-product of this economic necessity, it is necessary to inquire into the composition of the surplus labor army. What men form it? Why are they there? What do they do?

In the first place, since the workers must compete for employment, it inevitably follows that it is the fit and efficient who find employment. The skilled worker holds his place by virtue of his skill and efficiency. Were he less skilled, or were he unreliable or erratic, he would be swiftly replaced by a stronger competitor. The skilled and steady employments are not cumbered with clowns and idiots. A man finds his place according to his ability and the needs of the system, and those without ability, or incapable of satisfying the needs of the system, have no place. Thus, the poor telegrapher may develop into an excellent wood-chopper. But if the poor telegrapher cherishes the delusion that he is a good telegrapher, and at the same time disdains all other employments, he will have no employment at all, or he will be so poor at all other employments that he will work only now and again in lieu of better men. He will be among the first let off when times are dull, and among the last taken on when times are good. Or, to the point, he will be a member of the surplus labor army.

The Tramp

So the conclusion is reached that the less fit and less efficient, or the unfit and inefficient, compose the surplus labor army. Here are to be found the men who have tried and failed, the men who cannot hold jobs, —— the plumber apprentice who could not become a journeyman, and the plumber journeyman too clumsy and dull to retain employment; switchmen who wreck trains; clerks who cannot balance books; blacksmiths who lame horses; lawyers who cannot plead; in short, the failures of every trade and profession, and failures, many of them, in divers trades and professions. Failure is writ large, and in their wretchedness they bear the stamp of social disapprobation. Common work, any kind of work, wherever or however they can obtain it, is their portion.

But these hereditary inefficients do not alone compose the surplus labor army. There are the skilled but unsteady and unreliable men; and the old men, once skilled, but, with dwindling powers, no longer skilled.* And there are good men, too, splendidly skilled and efficient, but thrust out of the employment of dying or disaster-smitten industries. In this connection it is not out of place to note the misfortune of the workers in the British iron trades, who are suffering because of American inroads. And, last of all, are the unskilled laborers, the hewers of wood and drawers of water, the ditch-diggers, the men of pick and shovel, the helpers, lumpers, roustabouts. If trade is slack on a seacoast of two thousand miles, or the harvests are light in a great interior valley, myriads of these laborers lie idle, or make life miserable for their fellows in kindred unskilled employments.

*"Despondent and weary with vain attempts to struggle against an unsympathetic world, two old men were brought before Police Judge McHugh this afternoon to see whether some means could not be provided for their support, at least until springtime.

"George Westlake was the first one to receive the consideration of the court. Westlake is seventy-two years old. A charge of habitual drunkenness was placed against him, and he was sentenced to a term in the county jail, though it is more than probable that he was never under the influence of intoxicating liquor in his life. The act on the part of the authorities was one of kindness for him, as in the county jail he will be provided with a good place to sleep and plenty to eat.

"Joe Coat, aged sixty-nine years, will serve ninety days in the county jail for much the same reason as Westlake. He states that, if given a chance to do so, he will go out to a wood-camp and cut timber during the winter, but the police authorities realize that he could not long survive such a task." —— From the Butte (Montana) Miner, December 7th, 1904.

"'I end my life because I have reached the age limit, and there is no place for me in this world. Please notify my wife, No. 222 West 129th Street, New York.' Having summed up the cause of his despondency in this final message, James Hollander, fifty-six years old, shot himself through the left temple, in his room at the Stafford Hotel today." —— New York Herald.

25

The War of the Classes

A constant filtration goes on in the working world, and good material is continually drawn from the surplus labor army. Strikes and industrial dislocations shake up the workers, bring good men to the surface and sink men as good or not so good. The hope of the skilled striker is in that the scabs are less skilled, or less capable of becoming skilled; yet each strike attests to the efficiency that lurks beneath. After the Pullman strike, a few thousand railroad men were chagrined to find the work they had flung down taken up by men as good as themselves.

But one thing must be considered here. Under the present system, if the weakest and least fit were as strong and fit as the best, and the best were correspondingly stronger and fitter, the same condition would obtain. There would be the same army of employed labor, the same army of surplus labor. The whole thing is relative. There is no absolute standard of efficiency.

Comes now the tramp. And all conclusions may be anticipated by saying at once that he is a tramp because some one has to be a tramp. If he left the "road" and became a *very* efficient common laborer, some *ordinarily efficient* common laborer would have to take to the "road." The nooks and crannies are crowded by the surplus laborers; and when the first snow flies, and the tramps are driven into the cities, things become overcrowded and stringent police regulations are necessary.

The tramp is one of two kinds of men: he is either a discouraged worker or a discouraged criminal. Now a discouraged criminal, on investigation, proves to be a discouraged worker, or the descendant of discouraged workers; so that, in the last analysis, the tramp is a discouraged worker. Since there is not work for all, discouragement for some is unavoidable. How, then, does this process of discouragement operate?

The lower the employment in the industrial scale, the harder the conditions. The finer, the more delicate, the more skilled the trade, the higher is it lifted above the struggle. There is less pressure, less sordidness, less savagery. There are fewer glass-blowers proportionate to the needs of the glass-blowing industry than there are ditch-diggers proportionate to the needs of the ditch-digging industry. And not only this, for it requires a glass-blower to take the place of a striking glass-blower, while any kind of a striker or out-of-work can take the place of a ditch-digger. So the skilled trades are more independent, have more individuality and latitude. They may confer with their masters, make demands, assert themselves.

26

The Tramp

The unskilled laborers, on the other hand, have no voice in their affairs. The settlement of terms is none of their business. "Free contract" is all that remains to them. They may take what is offered, or leave it. There are plenty more of their kind. They do not count. They are members of the surplus labor army, and must be content with a hand-to-mouth existence.

The reward is likewise proportioned. The strong, fit worker in a skilled trade, where there is little labor pressure, is well compensated. He is a king compared with his less fortunate brothers in the unskilled occupations where the labor pressure is great. The mediocre worker not only is forced to be idle a large portion of the time, but when employed is forced to accept a pittance. A dollar a day on some days and nothing on other days will hardly support a man and wife and send children to school. And not only do the masters bear heavily upon him, and his own kind struggle for the morsel at his mouth, but all skilled and organized labor adds to his woe. Union men do not scab on one another, but in strikes, or when work is slack, it is considered "fair" for them to descend and take away the work of the common laborers. And take it away they do; for, as a matter of fact, a well-fed, ambitious machinist or a core-maker will transiently shovel coal better than an ill-fed, spiritless laborer.

Thus there is no encouragement for the unfit, inefficient, and mediocre. Their very inefficiency and mediocrity make them helpless as cattle and add to their misery. And the whole tendency for such is downward, until, at the bottom of the social pit, they are wretched, inarticulate beasts, living like beasts, breeding like beasts, dying like beasts. And how do they fare, these creatures born mediocre, whose heritage is neither brains nor brawn nor endurance? They are sweated in the slums in an atmosphere of discouragement and despair. There is no strength in weakness, no encouragement in foul air, vile food, and dank dens. They are there because they are so made that they are not fit to be higher up; but filth and obscenity do not strengthen the neck, nor does chronic emptiness of belly stiffen the back.

For the mediocre there is no hope. Mediocrity is a sin. Poverty is the penalty of failure, — poverty, from whose loins spring the criminal and the tramp, both failures, both discouraged workers. Poverty is the inferno where ignorance festers and vice corrodes, and where the physical, mental, and moral parts of nature are aborted and denied.

That the charge of rashness in splashing the picture be not

The War of the Classes

incurred, let the following authoritative evidence be considered: first, the work and wages of mediocrity and inefficiency, and, second, the habitat:

The New York Sun of February 28, 1901, describes the opening of a factory in New York City by the American Tobacco Company. Cheroots were to be made in this factory in competition with other factories which refused to be absorbed by the trust. The trust advertised for girls. The crowd of men and boys who wanted work was so great in front of the building that the police were forced with their clubs to clear them away. The wage paid the girls was $2.50 per week, sixty cents of which went for car fare.*

Miss Nellie Mason Auten, a graduate student of the department of sociology at the University of Chicago, recently made a thorough investigation of the garment trades of Chicago. Her figures were published in the American Journal of Sociology, and commented upon by the Literary Digest. She found women working ten hours a day, six days a week, for forty cents per week (a rate of two-thirds of a cent an hour). Many women earned less than a dollar a week, and none of them worked every week. The following table will best summarize Miss Auten's investigations among a portion of the garment-workers:

Industry	Average Individual Weekly Wages	Average Number of Weeks Employed	Average Yearly Earnings
Dressmakers	$ .90	42.	$37.00
Pants-Finishers	1.31	27.58	42.41
Housewives and Pants-Finishers	1.58	30.21	47.49
Seamstresses	2.03	32.78	64.10
Pants-makers	2.13	30.77	75.61
Miscellaneous	2.77	29.	81.80
Tailors	6.22	31.96	211.92
General Averages	2.48	31.18	76.74

*In the San Francisco Examiner of November 16, 1904, there is an account of the use of fire-hose to drive away three hundred men who wanted work at unloading a vessel in the harbor. So anxious were the men to get the two or three hours' job that they made a veritable mob and had to be driven off.

The Tramp

Walter A. Wyckoff, who is as great an authority upon the worker as Josiah Flynt is on the tramp, furnishes the following Chicago experience:

"Many of the men were so weakened by the want and hardship of the winter that they were no longer in condition for effective labor. Some of the bosses who were in need of added hands were obliged to turn men away because of physical incapacity. One instance of this I shall not soon forget. It was when I overheard, early one morning at a factory gate, an interview between a would-be laborer and the boss. I knew the applicant for a Russian Jew, who had at home an old mother and a wife and two young children to support. He had had intermittent employment throughout the winter in a sweater's den,* barely enough to keep them all alive, and, after the hardships of the cold season, he was again in desperate straits for work.

"The boss had all but agreed to take him on for some sort of unskilled labor, when, struck by the cadaverous look of the man, he told him to bare his arm. Up went the sleeve of his coat and his ragged flannel shirt, exposing a naked arm with the muscles nearly gone, and the blue-white transparent skin stretched over sinews and the outlines of the bones. Pitiful beyond words was his effort to give a semblance of strength to the biceps which rose faintly to the upward movement of the forearm. But the boss sent him off with an oath and a contemptuous laugh; and I watched the fellow as he turned down the street, facing the fact of his starving family with a despair at his heart which only mortal man can feel and no mortal tongue can speak."

Concerning habitat, Mr. Jacob Riis has stated that in New York City, in the block bounded by Stanton, Houston, Attorney, and Ridge streets, the size of which is 200 by 300, there is a warren of 2244 human beings.

In the block bounded by Sixty-first and Sixty-second streets, and Amsterdam and West End avenues, are over four thousand human creatures, — quite a comfortable New England village to crowd into one city block.

*"It was no uncommon thing in these sweatshops for men to sit bent over a sewing-machine continuously from eleven to fifteen hours a day in July weather, operating a sewing-machine by foot-power, and often so driven that they could not stop for lunch. The seasonal character of the work meant demoralizing toil for a few months in the year, and a not less demoralizing idleness for the remainder of the time. Consumption, the plague of the tenements and the especial plague of the garment industry, carried off many of these workers; poor nutrition and exhaustion, many more." — From McClure's Magazine.

The War of the Classes

The Rev. Dr. Behrends, speaking of the block bounded by Canal, Hester, Eldridge, and Forsyth streets, says: "In a room 12 by 8 and 5.5 feet high, it was found that nine persons slept and prepared their food. . . . In another room, located in a dark cellar, without screens or partitions, were together two men with their wives and a girl of fourteen, two single men and a boy of seventeen, two women and four boys, — nine, ten, eleven, and fifteen years old, — fourteen persons in all."

Here humanity rots. Its victims, with grim humor, call it "tenant-house rot." Or, as a legislative report puts it: "Here infantile life unfolds its bud, but perishes before its first anniversary. Here youth is ugly with loathsome disease, and the deformities which follow physical degeneration."

These are the men and women who are what they are because they were not better born, or because they happened to be unluckily born in time and space. Gauged by the needs of the system, they are weak and worthless. The hospital and the pauper's grave await them, and they offer no encouragement to the mediocre worker who has failed higher up in the industrial structure. Such a worker, conscious that he has failed, conscious from the hard fact that he cannot obtain work in the higher employments, finds several courses open to him. He may come down and be a beast in the social pit, for instance; but if he be of a certain caliber, the effect of the social pit will be to discourage him from work. In his blood a rebellion will quicken, and he will elect to become either a felon or a tramp.

If he have fought the hard fight he is not unacquainted with the lure of the "road." When out of work and still undiscouraged, he has been forced to "hit the road" between large cities in his quest for a job. He has loafed, seen the country and green things, laughed in joy, lain on his back and listened to the birds singing overhead, unannoyed by factory whistles and bosses' harsh commands; and, most significant of all, *he has lived!* That is the point! He has not starved to death. Not only has he been care-free and happy, but he has lived! And from the knowledge that he has idled and is still alive, he achieves a new outlook on life; and the more he experiences the unenviable lot of the poor worker, the more the blandishments of the "road" take hold of him. And finally he flings his challenge in the face of society, imposes a valorous boycott on all work, and joins the far-wanderers of Hoboland, the gypsy folk of this latter day.

But the tramp does not usually come from the slums. His place

30

of birth is ordinarily a bit above, and sometimes a very great bit above. A confessed failure, he yet refuses to accept the punishment, and swerves aside from the slum to vagabondage. The average beast in the social pit is either too much of a beast, or too much of a slave to the bourgeois ethics and ideals of his masters, to manifest this flicker of rebellion. But the social pit, out of its discouragement and viciousness, breeds criminals, men who prefer being beasts of prey to being beasts of work. And the mediocre criminal, in turn, the unfit and inefficient criminal, is discouraged by the strong arm of the law and goes over to trampdom.

These men, the discouraged worker and the discouraged criminal, voluntarily withdraw themselves from the struggle for work. Industry does not need them. There are no factories shut down through lack of labor, no projected railroads unbuilt for want of pick-and-shovel men. Women are still glad to toil for a dollar a week, and men and boys to clamor and fight for work at the factory gates. No one misses these discouraged men, and in going away they have made it somewhat easier for those that remain.

So the case stands thus: There being more men than there is work for men to do, a surplus labor army inevitably results. The surplus labor army is an economic necessity; without it, present society would fall to pieces. Into the surplus labor army are herded the mediocre, the inefficient, the unfit, and those incapable of satisfying the industrial needs of the system. The struggle for work between the members of the surplus labor army is sordid and savage, and at the bottom of the social pit the struggle is vicious and beastly. This struggle tends to discouragement, and the victims of this discouragement are the criminal and the tramp. The tramp is not an economic necessity such as the surplus labor army, but he is the by-product of an economic necessity.

The "road" is one of the safety-valves through which the waste of the social organism is given off. And *being given off* constitutes the negative function of the tramp. Society, as at present organized, makes much waste of human life. This waste must be eliminated. Chloroform or electrocution would be a simple, merciful solution of this problem of elimination; but the ruling ethics, while permitting the human waste, will not permit a humane elimination of that waste. This paradox demonstrates the irreconcilability of theoretical ethics and industrial need.

And so the tramp becomes self-eliminating. And not only self! Since he is manifestly unfit for things as they are, and since kind is prone to beget kind, it is necessary that his kind cease with him, that his progeny shall not be, that he play the eunuch's part in this twentieth century after Christ. And he plays it. He does not breed. Sterility is his portion, as it is the portion of the woman on the street. They might have been mates, but society has decreed otherwise.

And, while it is not nice that these men should die, it is ordained that they must die, and we should not quarrel with them if they cumber our highways and kitchen stoops with their perambulating carcasses. This is a form of elimination we not only countenance but compel. Therefore let us be cheerful and honest about it. Let us be as stringent as we please with our police regulations, but for goodness' sake let us refrain from telling the tramp to go to work. Not only is it unkind, but it is untrue and hypocritical. We know there is no work for him. As the scapegoat to our economic and industrial sinning, or to the plan of things, if you will, we should give him credit. Let us be just. He is so made. Society made him. He did not make himself.

The Scab

IN a competitive society, where men struggle with one another for food and shelter, what is more natural than that generosity, when it diminishes the food and shelter of men other than he who is generous, should be held an accursed thing? Wise old saws to the contrary, he who takes from a man's purse takes from his existence. To strike at a man's food and shelter is to strike at his life; and in a society organized on a tooth-and-nail basis, such an act, performed though it may be under the guise of generosity, is none the less menacing and terrible.

It is for this reason that a laborer is so fiercely hostile to another laborer who offers to work for less pay or longer hours. To hold his place, (which is to live), he must offset this offer by another equally liberal, which is equivalent to giving away somewhat from the food and shelter he enjoys. To sell his day's work for $2, instead of $2.50, means that he, his wife, and his children will not have so good a roof over their heads, so warm clothes on their backs, so substantial food in their stomachs. Meat will be bought less frequently and it will be tougher and less nutritious, stout new shoes will go less often on the children's feet, and disease and death will be more imminent in a cheaper house and neighborhood.

Thus the generous laborer, giving more of a day's work for less return, (measured in terms of food and shelter), threatens the life of his less generous brother laborer, and at the best, if he does not destroy that life, he diminishes it. Whereupon the less generous laborer looks upon him as an enemy, and, as men are inclined to do in a tooth-and-nail society, he tries to kill the man who is trying to kill him.

When a striker kills with a brick the man who has taken his place, he has no sense of wrong-doing. In the deepest holds of his being, though he does not reason the impulse, he has an ethical sanction. He feels dimly that he has justification, just as the home-defending Boer felt, though more sharply, with each bullet he fired at the invading English. Behind every brick thrown by a striker is the selfish will "to live" of himself, and the slightly altruistic will "to live" of his family. The family group came into the world before the State group, and society, being still on the primitive basis of tooth and nail, the will "to live" of the State is not so

The War of the Classes

compelling to the striker as is the will "to live" of his family and himself.

In addition to the use of bricks, clubs, and bullets, the selfish laborer finds it necessary to express his feelings in speech. Just as the peaceful country-dweller calls the sea-rover a "pirate," and the stout burgher calls the man who breaks into his strong-box a "robber," so the selfish laborer applies the opprobrious epithet a "scab" to the laborer who takes from him food and shelter by being more generous in the disposal of his labor power. The sentimental connotation of "scab" is as terrific as that of "traitor" or "Judas," and a sentimental definition would be as deep and varied as the human heart. It is far easier to arrive at what may be called a technical definition, worded in commercial terms, as, for instance, that *a scab is one who gives more value for the same price than another.*

The laborer who gives more time or strength or skill for the same wage than another, or equal time or strength or skill for a less wage, is a scab. This generousness on his part is hurtful to his fellow-laborers, for it compels them to an equal generousness which is not to their liking, and which gives them less of food and shelter. But a word may be said for the scab. Just as his act makes his rivals compulsorily generous, so do they, by fortune of birth and training, make compulsory his act of generousness. He does not scab because he wants to scab. No whim of the spirit, no burgeoning of the heart, leads him to give more of his labor power than they for a certain sum.

It is because he cannot get work on the same terms as they that he is a scab. There is less work than there are men to do work. This is patent, else the scab would not loom so large on the labor-market horizon. Because they are stronger than he, or more skilled, or more energetic, it is impossible for him to take their places at the same wage. To take their places he must give more value, must work longer hours or receive a smaller wage. He does so, and he cannot help it, for his will "to live" is driving him on as well as they are being driven on by their will "to live"; and to live he must win food and shelter, which he can do only by receiving permission to work from some man who owns a bit of land or a piece of machinery. And to receive permission from this man, he must make the transaction profitable for him.

Viewed in this light, the scab, who gives more labor power for a certain price than his fellows, is not so generous after all. He is no more generous with his energy than the chattel slave and the convict

34

The Scab

laborer, who, by the way, are the almost perfect scabs. They give their labor power for about the minimum possible price. But, within limits, they may loaf and malinger, and, as scabs, are exceeded by the machine, which never loafs and malingers and which is the ideally perfect scab.

It is not nice to be a scab. Not only is it not in good social taste and comradeship, but, from the standpoint of food and shelter, it is bad business policy. Nobody desires to scab, to give most for least. The ambition of every individual is quite the opposite, to give least for most; and, as a result, living in a tooth-and-nail society, battle royal is waged by the ambitious individuals. But in its most salient aspect, that of the struggle over the division of the joint product, it is no longer a battle between individuals, but between groups of individuals. Capital and labor apply themselves to raw material, make something useful out of it, add to its value, and then proceed to quarrel over the division of the added value. Neither cares to give most for least. Each is intent on giving less than the other and on receiving more.

Labor combines into its unions, capital into partnerships, associations, corporations, and trusts. A group-struggle is the result, in which the individuals, as individuals, play no part. The Brotherhood of Carpenters and Joiners, for instance, serves notice on the Master Builders' Association that it demands an increase of the wage of its members from $3.50 a day to $4, and a Saturday half-holiday without pay. This means that the carpenters are trying to give less for more. Where they received $21 for six full days, they are endeavoring to get $22 for five days and a half, — that is, they will work half a day less each week and receive a dollar more.

Also, they expect the Saturday half-holiday to give work to one additional man for each eleven previously employed. This last affords a splendid example of the development of the group idea. In this particular struggle the individual has no chance at all for life. The individual carpenter would be crushed like a mote by the Master Builders' Association, and like a mote the individual master builder would be crushed by the Brotherhood of Carpenters and Joiners.

In the group-struggle over the division of the joint product, labor utilizes the union with its two great weapons, the strike and the boycott; while capital utilizes the trust and the association, the weapons of which are the black-list, the lockout, and the scab. The scab is by far the most formidable weapon of the three. He is the

35

man who breaks strikes and causes all the trouble. Without him there would be no trouble, for the strikers are willing to remain out peacefully and indefinitely so long as other men are not in their places, and so long as the particular aggregation of capital with which they are fighting is eating its head off in enforced idleness.

But both warring groups have reserve weapons. Were it not for the scab, these weapons would not be brought into play. But the scab takes the place of the striker, who begins at once to wield a most powerful weapon, terrorism. The will "to live" of the scab recoils from the menace of broken bones and violent death. With all due respect to the labor leaders, who are not to be blamed for volubly asseverating otherwise, terrorism is a well-defined and eminently successful policy of the labor unions. It has probably won them more strikes than all the rest of the weapons in their arsenal. This terrorism, however, must be clearly understood. It is directed solely against the scab, placing him in such fear for life and limb as to drive him out of the contest. But when terrorism gets out of hand and inoffensive non-combatants are injured, law and order threatened, and property destroyed, it becomes an edged tool that cuts both ways. This sort of terrorism is sincerely deplored by the labor leaders, for it has probably lost them as many strikes as have been lost by any other single cause.

The scab is powerless under terrorism. As a rule, he is not so good nor gritty a man as the men he is displacing, and he lacks their fighting organization. He stands in dire need of stiffening and backing. His employers, the capitalists, draw their two remaining weapons, the ownership of which is debatable, but which they for the time being happen to control. These two weapons may be called the political and judicial machinery of society. When the scab crumples up and is ready to go down before the fists, bricks, and bullets of the labor group, the capitalist group puts the police and soldiers into the field, and begins a general bombardment of injunctions. Victory usually follows, for the labor group cannot withstand the combined assault of gatling guns and injunctions.

But it has been noted that the ownership of the political and judicial machinery of society is debatable. In the Titanic struggle over the division of the joint product, each group reaches out for every available weapon. Nor are they blinded by the smoke of conflict. They fight their battles as coolly and collectedly as ever battles were fought on paper. The capitalist group has long since

The Scab

realized the immense importance of controlling the political and judicial machinery of society.

Taught by gatlings and injunctions, which have smashed many an otherwise successful strike, the labor group is beginning to realize that it all depends upon who is behind and who is before the gatlings and the injunctions. And he who knows the labor movement knows that there is slowly growing up and being formulated a clear and definite policy for the capture of the political and judicial machinery.

This is the terrible spectre which Mr. John Graham Brooks sees looming portentously over the twentieth century world. No man may boast a more intimate knowledge of the labor movement than he; and he reiterates again and again the dangerous likelihood of the whole labor group capturing the political machinery of society. As he says in his recent book:* "It is not probable that employers can destroy unionism in the United States. Adroit and desperate attempts will, however, be made, if we mean by unionism the undisciplined and aggressive fact of vigorous and determined organizations. If capital should prove too strong in this struggle, the result is easy to predict. The employers have only to convince organized labor that it cannot hold its own against the capitalist manager, and the whole energy that now goes to the union will turn to an aggressive political socialism. It will not be the harmless sympathy with increased city and state functions which trade unions already feel; it will become a turbulent political force bent upon using every weapon of taxation against the rich."

This struggle not to be a scab, to avoid giving more for less and to succeed in giving less for more, is more vital than it would appear on the surface. The capitalist and labor groups are locked together in desperate battle, and neither side is swayed by moral considerations more than skin-deep. The labor group hires business agents, lawyers, and organizers, and is beginning to intimidate legislators by the strength of its solid vote; and more directly, in the near future, it will attempt to control legislation by capturing it bodily through the ballot-box. On the other hand, the capitalist group, numerically weaker, hires newspapers, universities, and legislatures, and strives to bend to its need all the forces which go to mould public opinion.

The only honest morality displayed by either side is white-hot

*The Social Unrest. Macmillan Company.

The War of the Classes

indignation at the iniquities of the other side. The striking teamster complacently takes a scab driver into an alley, and with an iron bar breaks his arms, so that he can drive no more, but cries out to high Heaven for justice when the capitalist breaks his skull by means of a club in the hands of a policeman. Nay, the members of a union will declaim in impassioned rhetoric for the God-given right of an eight-hour day, and at the time be working their own business agent seventeen hours out of the twenty-four.

A capitalist such as Collis P. Huntington, and his name is Legion, after a long life spent in buying the aid of countless legislatures, will wax virtuously wrathful, and condemn in unmeasured terms "the dangerous tendency of crying out to the Government for aid" in the way of labor legislation. Without a quiver, a member of the capitalist group will run tens of thousands of pitiful child-laborers through his life-destroying cotton factories, and weep maudlin and constitutional tears over one scab hit in the back with a brick. He will drive a "compulsory" free contract with an unorganized laborer on the basis of a starvation wage, saying, "Take it or leave it," knowing that to leave it means to die of hunger, and in the next breath, when the organizer entices that laborer into a union, will storm patriotically about the inalienable right of all men to work. In short, the chief moral concern of either side is with the morals of the other side. They are not in the business for their moral welfare, but to achieve the enviable position of the non-scab who gets more than he gives.

But there is more to the question than has yet been discussed. The labor scab is no more detestable to his brother laborers than is the capitalist scab to his brother capitalists. A capitalist may get most for least in dealing with his laborers, and in so far be a non-scab; but at the same time, in his dealings with his fellow-capitalists, he may give most for least and be the very worst kind of scab. The most heinous crime an employer of labor can commit is to scab on his fellow-employers of labor. Just as the individual laborers have organized into groups to protect themselves from the peril of the scab laborer, so have the employers organized into groups to protect themselves from the peril of the scab employer. The employers' federations, associations, and trusts are nothing more nor less than unions. They are organized to destroy scabbing amongst themselves and to encourage scabbing amongst others. For this reason they pool interests, determine prices, and present an unbroken and aggressive front to the labor group.

The Scab

As has been said before, nobody likes to play the compulsorily generous role of scab. It is a bad business proposition on the face of it. And it is patent that there would be no capitalist scabs if there were not more capital than there is work for capital to do. When there are enough factories in existence to supply, with occasional stoppages, a certain commodity, the building of new factories by a rival concern, for the production of that commodity, is plain advertisement that that capital is out of a job. The first act of this new aggregation of capital will be to cut prices, to give more for less, — in short to scab, to strike at the very existence of the less generous aggregation of capital the work of which it is trying to do.

No scab capitalist strives to give more for less for any other reason than that he hopes, by undercutting a competitor and driving that competitor out of the market, to get that market and its profits for himself. His ambition is to achieve the day when he shall stand alone in the field both as buyer and seller, — when he will be the royal non-scab, buying most for least, selling least for most, and reducing all about him, the small buyers and sellers, (the consumers and the laborers), to a general condition of scabdom. This, for example, has been the history of Mr. Rockefeller and the Standard Oil Company. Through all the sordid villanies of scabdom he has passed, until today he is a most regal non-scab. However, to continue in this enviable position, he must be prepared at a moment's notice to go scabbing again. And he is prepared. Whenever a competitor arises, Mr. Rockefeller changes about from giving least for most and gives most for least with such a vengeance as to drive the competitor out of existence.

The banded capitalists discriminate against a scab capitalist by refusing him trade advantages, and by combining against him in most relentless fashion. The banded laborers, discriminating against a scab laborer in more primitive fashion, with a club, are no more merciless than the banded capitalists.

Mr. Casson tells of a New York capitalist who withdrew from the Sugar Union several years ago and became a scab. He was worth something like twenty millions of dollars. But the Sugar Union, standing shoulder to shoulder with the Railroad Union and several other unions, beat him to his knees till he cried, "Enough." So frightfully did they beat him that he was obliged to turn over to his creditors his home, his chickens, and his gold watch. In point of fact, he was as thoroughly bludgeoned by the Federation of Capitalist Unions as ever scab workman was bludgeoned by a labor

The War of the Classes

union. The intent in either case is the same, — to destroy the scab's producing power. The labor scab with concussion of the brain is put out of business, and so is the capitalist scab who has lost all his dollars down to his chickens and his watch.

But the role of scab passes beyond the individual. Just as individuals scab on other individuals, so do groups scab on other groups. And the principle involved is precisely the same as in the case of the simple labor scab. A group, in the nature of its organization, is often compelled to give most for least, and, so doing, to strike at the life of another group. At the present moment all Europe is appalled by that colossal scab, the United States. And Europe is clamorous with agitation for a Federation of National Unions to protect her from the United States. It may be remarked, in passing, that in its prime essentials this agitation in no wise differs from the trade-union agitation among workmen in any industry. The trouble is caused by the scab who is giving most for least. The result of the American scab's nefarious actions will be to strike at the food and shelter of Europe. The way for Europe to protect herself is to quit bickering among her parts and to form a union against the scab. And if the union is formed, armies and navies may be expected to be brought into play in fashion similar to the bricks and clubs in ordinary labor struggles.

In this connection, and as one of many walking delegates for the nations, M. Leroy-Beaulieu, the noted French economist, may well be quoted. In a letter to the Vienna Tageblatt, he advocates an economic alliance among the Continental nations for the purpose of barring out American goods, an economic alliance, in his own language, " *which may possibly and desirably develop into a political alliance.*"

It will be noted, in the utterances of the Continental walking delegates, that, one and all, they leave England out of the proposed union. And in England herself the feeling is growing that her days are numbered if she cannot unite for offence and defence with the great American scab. As Andrew Carnegie said some time ago, "The only course for Great Britain seems to be reunion with her grandchild or sure decline to a secondary place, and then to comparative insignificance in the future annals of the English-speaking race."

Cecil Rhodes, speaking of what would have obtained but for the pig-headedness of George III, and of what will obtain when England and the United States are united, said, *"No cannon would...*

The Scab

Be fired on either hemisphere but by permission of the english race. " It would seem that England, fronted by the hostile Continental Union and flanked by the great American scab, has nothing left but to join with the scab and play the historic labor role of armed Pinkerton. Granting the words of Cecil Rhodes, the United States would be enabled to scab without let or hindrance on Europe, while England, as professional strike-breaker and policeman, destroyed the unions and kept order.

All this may appear fantastic and erroneous, but there is in it a soul of truth vastly more significant than it may seem. Civilization may be expressed today in terms of trade-unionism. Individual struggles have largely passed away, but group-struggles increase prodigiously. And the things for which the groups struggle are the same as of old. Shorn of all subtleties and complexities, the chief struggle of men, and of groups of men, is for food and shelter. And, as of old they struggled with tooth and nail, so today they struggle with teeth and nails elongated into armies and navies, machines, and economic advantages.

Under the definition that a scab is *one who gives more value for the same price than another,* it would seem that society can be generally divided into the two classes of the scabs and the non-scabs. But on closer investigation, however, it will be seen that the non-scab is a vanishing quantity. In the social jungle, everybody is preying upon everybody else. As in the case of Mr. Rockefeller, he who was a scab yesterday is a non-scab today, and tomorrow may be a scab again.

The woman stenographer or book-keeper who receives forty dollars per month where a man was receiving seventy-five is a scab. So is the woman who does a man's work at a weaving-machine, and the child who goes into the mill or factory. And the father, who is scabbed out of work by the wives and children of other men, sends his own wife and children to scab in order to save himself.

When a publisher offers an author better royalties than other publishers have been paying him, he is scabbing on those other publishers. The reporter on a newspaper, who feels he should be receiving a larger salary for his work, says so, and is shown the door, is replaced by a reporter who is a scab; whereupon, when the belly-need presses, the displaced reporter goes to another paper and scabs himself. The minister who hardens his heart to a call, and waits for a certain congregation to offer him say $500 a year more, often finds himself scabbed upon by another and more impecunious minister; and the next time it is *his* turn to scab while a brother minister is hardening his heart to a call. The scab is everywhere. The professional strike-breakers, who as a class receive large wages, will scab on one another, while scab unions are even formed to prevent scabbing upon scabs.

There are non-scabs, but they are usually born so, and are protected by the whole might of society in the possession of their food and shelter. King Edward is such a type, as are all individuals who receive hereditary food-and-shelter privileges, — such as the present Duke of Bedford, for instance, who yearly receives $75,000 from the good people of London because some former king gave some former ancestor of his the market privileges of Covent Garden. The irresponsible rich are likewise non-scabs, — and by them is meant that coupon-clipping class which hires its managers and brains to invest the money usually left it by its ancestors.

Outside these lucky creatures, all the rest, at one time or another in their lives, are scabs, at one time or another are engaged in giving more for a certain price than any one else. The meek professor in some endowed institution, by his meek suppression of his convictions, is giving more for his salary than gave the other and more outspoken professor whose chair he occupies. And when a political party dangles a full dinner-pail in the eyes of the toiling masses, it is offering more for a vote than the dubious dollar of the opposing party. Even a money-lender is not above taking a slightly lower rate of interest and saying nothing about it.

Such is the tangle of conflicting interests in a tooth-and-nail society that people cannot avoid being scabs, are often made so against their desires, and are often unconsciously made so. When several trades in a certain locality demand and receive an advance in wages, they are unwittingly making scabs of their fellow-laborers in that district who have received no advance in wages. In San Francisco the barbers, laundry-workers, and milk-wagon drivers received such an advance in wages. Their employers promptly added the amount of this advance to the selling price of their wares. The price of shaves, of washing, and of milk went up. This reduced the purchasing power of the unorganized laborers, and, in point of fact, reduced their wages and made them greater scabs.

Because the British laborer is disinclined to scab, — that is, because he restricts his output in order to give less for the wage he receives, — it is to a certain extent made possible for the American capitalist, who receives a less restricted output from his laborers, to

The Scab

play the scab on the English capitalist. As a result of this, (of course combined with other causes), the American capitalist and the American laborer are striking at the food and shelter of the English capitalist and laborer.

The English laborer is starving today because, among other things, he is not a scab. He practises the policy of "ca' canny," which may be defined as "go easy." In order to get most for least, in many trades he performs but from one-fourth to one-sixth of the labor he is well able to perform. An instance of this is found in the building of the Westinghouse Electric Works at Manchester. The British limit per man was 400 bricks per day. The Westinghouse Company imported a "driving" American contractor, aided by half a dozen "driving" American foremen, and the British bricklayer swiftly attained an average of 1800 bricks per day, with a maximum of 2500 bricks for the plainest work.

But, the British laborer's policy of "ca' canny," which is the very honorable one of giving least for most, and which is likewise the policy of the English capitalist, is nevertheless frowned upon by the English capitalist, whose business existence is threatened by the great American scab. From the rise of the factory system, the English capitalist gladly embraced the opportunity, wherever he found it, of giving least for most. He did it all over the world whenever he enjoyed a market monopoly, and he did it at home with the laborers employed in his mills, destroying them like flies till prevented, within limits, by the passage of the Factory Acts. Some of the proudest fortunes of England today may trace their origin to the giving of least for most to the miserable slaves of the factory towns. But at the present time the English capitalist is outraged because his laborers are employing against him precisely the same policy he employed against them, and which he would employ again did the chance present itself.

Yet "ca' canny" is a disastrous thing to the British laborer. It has driven ship-building from England to Scotland, bottle-making from Scotland to Belgium, flint-glass-making from England to Germany, and today is steadily driving industry after industry to other countries. A correspondent from Northampton wrote not long ago: "Factories are working half and third time. . . . There is no strike, there is no real labor trouble, but the masters and men are alike suffering from sheer lack of employment. Markets which were once theirs are now American." It would seem that the unfortunate British laborer is 'twixt the devil and the deep sea.

The War of the Classes

If he gives most for least, he faces a frightful slavery such as marked the beginning of the factory system. If he gives least for most, he drives industry away to other countries and has no work at all.

But the union laborers of the United States have nothing of which to boast, while, according to their trade-union ethics, they have a great deal of which to be ashamed. They passionately preach short hours and big wages, the shorter the hours and the bigger the wages the better. Their hatred for a scab is as terrible as the hatred of a patriot for a traitor, of a Christian for a Judas. And in the face of all this, they are as colossal scabs as the United States is a colossal scab. For all of their boasted unions and high labor ideals, they are about the most thoroughgoing scabs on the planet.

Receiving $4.50 per day, because of his proficiency and immense working power, the American laborer has been known to scab upon scabs (so called) who took his place and received only $0.90 per day for a longer day. In this particular instance, five Chinese coolies, working longer hours, gave less value for the price received from their employer than did one American laborer.

It is upon his brother laborers overseas that the American laborer most outrageously scabs. As Mr. Casson has shown, an English nail-maker gets $3 per week, while an American nail-maker gets $30. But the English worker turns out 200 pounds of nails per week, while the American turns out 5500 pounds. If he were as "fair" as his English brother, other things being equal, he would be receiving, at the English worker's rate of pay, $82.50. As it is, he is scabbing upon his English brother to the tune of $79.50 per week. Dr. Schultze-Gaevernitz has shown that a German weaver produces 466 yards of cotton a week at a cost of .303 per yard, while an American weaver produces 1200 yards at a cost of .02 per yard.

But, it may be objected, a great part of this is due to the more improved American machinery. Very true, but none the less a great part is still due to the superior energy, skill, and willingness of the American laborer. The English laborer is faithful to the policy of "ca' canny." He refuses point-blank to get the work out of a machine that the New World scab gets out of a machine. Mr. Maxim, observing a wasteful hand-labor process in his English factory, invented a machine which he proved capable of displacing several men. But workman after workman was put at the machine, and without exception they turned out neither more nor less than a workman turned out by hand. They obeyed the mandate of the

The Scab

union and went easy, while Mr. Maxim gave up in despair. Nor will the British workman run machines at as high speed as the American, nor will he run so many. An American workman will "give equal attention simultaneously to three, four, or six machines or tools, while the British workman is compelled by his trade union to limit his attention to one, so that employment may be given to half a dozen men."

But for scabbing, no blame attaches itself anywhere. With rare exceptions, all the people in the world are scabs. The strong, capable workman gets a job and holds it because of his strength and capacity. And he holds it because out of his strength and capacity he gives a better value for his wage than does the weaker and less capable workman. Therefore he is scabbing upon his weaker and less capable brother workman. He is giving more value for the price paid by the employer.

The superior workman scabs upon the inferior workman because he is so constituted and cannot help it. The one, by fortune of birth and upbringing, is strong and capable; the other, by fortune of birth and upbringing, is not so strong nor capable. It is for the same reason that one country scabs upon another. That country which has the good fortune to possess great natural resources, a finer sun and soil, unhampering institutions, and a deft and intelligent labor class and capitalist class is bound to scab upon a country less fortunately situated. It is the good fortune of the United States that is making her the colossal scab, just as it is the good fortune of one man to be born with a straight back while his brother is born with a hump.

It is not good to give most for least, not good to be a scab. The word has gained universal opprobrium. On the other hand, to be a non-scab, to give least for most, is universally branded as stingy, selfish, and unchristian-like. So all the world, like the British workman, is 'twixt the devil and the deep sea. It is treason to one's fellows to scab, it is unchristian-like not to scab.

Since to give least for most, and to give most for least, are universally bad, what remains? Equity remains, which is to give like for like, the same for the same, neither more nor less. But this equity, society, as at present constituted, cannot give. It is not in the nature of present-day society for men to give like for like, the same for the same. And so long as men continue to live in this competitive society, struggling tooth and nail with one another for food and shelter, (which is to struggle tooth and nail with one another for

45

life), that long will the scab continue to exist. His will "to live" will force him to exist. He may be flouted and jeered by his brothers, he may be beaten with bricks and clubs by the men who by superior strength and capacity scab upon him as he scabs upon them by longer hours and smaller wages, but through it all he will persist, giving a bit more of most for least than they are giving.

The Question of the Maximum

FOR any social movement or development there must be a maximum limit beyond which it cannot proceed. That civilization which does not advance must decline, and so, when the maximum of development has been reached in any given direction, society must either retrograde or change the direction of its advance. There are many families of men that have failed, in the critical period of their economic evolution, to effect a change in direction, and were forced to fall back. Vanquished at the moment of their maximum, they have dropped out of the whirl of the world. There was no room for them. Stronger competitors have taken their places, and they have either rotted into oblivion or remain to be crushed under the iron heel of the dominant races in as remorseless a struggle as the world has yet witnessed. But in this struggle fair women and chivalrous men will play no part. Types and ideals have changed. Helens and Launcelots are anachronisms. Blows will be given and taken, and men fight and die, but not for faiths and altars. Shrines will be desecrated, but they will be the shrines, not of temples, but market-places. Prophets will arise, but they will be the prophets of prices and products. Battles will be waged, not for honor and glory, nor for thrones and sceptres, but for dollars and cents and for marts and exchanges. Brain and not brawn will endure, and the captains of war will be commanded by the captains of industry. In short, it will be a contest for the mastery of the world's commerce and for industrial supremacy.

It is more significant, this struggle into which we have plunged, for the fact that it is the first struggle to involve the globe. No general movement of man has been so wide-spreading, so far-reaching. Quite local was the supremacy of any ancient people; likewise the rise to empire of Macedonia and Rome, the waves of Arabian valor and fanaticism, and the mediaeval crusades to the Holy Sepulchre. But since those times the planet has undergone a unique shrinkage.

The world of Homer, limited by the coast-lines of the Mediterranean and Black seas, was a far vaster world than ours of today, which we weigh, measure, and compute as accurately and as easily as if it were a child's play-ball. Steam has made its parts accessible and drawn them closer together. The telegraph annihilates space and time. Each morning, every part knows what every other part is

47

The War of the Classes

thinking, contemplating, or doing. A discovery in a German laboratory is being demonstrated in San Francisco within twenty-four hours. A book written in South Africa is published by simultaneous copyright in every English-speaking country, and on the day following is in the hands of the translators. The death of an obscure missionary in China, or of a whiskey-smuggler in the South Seas, is served, the world over, with the morning toast. The wheat output of Argentine or the gold of Klondike are known wherever men meet and trade. Shrinkage, or centralization, has become such that the humblest clerk in any metropolis may place his hand on the pulse of the world. The planet has indeed grown very small; and because of this, no vital movement can remain in the clime or country where it takes its rise.

And so today the economic and industrial impulse is world-wide. It is a matter of import to every people. None may be careless of it. To do so is to perish. It is become a battle, the fruits of which are to the strong, and to none but the strongest of the strong. As the movement approaches its maximum, centralization accelerates and competition grows keener and closer. The competitor nations cannot all succeed. So long as the movement continues its present direction, not only will there not be room for all, but the room that is will become less and less; and when the moment of the maximum is at hand, there will be no room at all. Capitalistic production will have overreached itself, and a change of direction will then be inevitable.

Divers queries arise: What is the maximum of commercial development the world can sustain? How far can it be exploited? How much capital is necessary? Can sufficient capital be accumulated? A brief resume of the industrial history of the last one hundred years or so will be relevant at this stage of the discussion. Capitalistic production, in its modern significance, was born of the industrial revolution in England in the latter half of the eighteenth century. The great inventions of that period were both its father and its mother, while, as Mr. Brooks Adams has shown, the looted treasure of India was the potent midwife. Had there not been an unwonted increase of capital, the impetus would not have been given to invention, while even steam might have languished for generations instead of at once becoming, as it did, the most prominent factor in the new method of production. The improved application of these inventions in the first decades of the nineteenth century mark the transition from the domestic to the factory system of manufacture and inaugurated the era of capitalism. The magnitude of this revolution is manifested by the fact that England alone had invented the means and equipped herself with the machinery whereby she could overstock the world's markets. The home market could not consume a tithe of the home product. To manufacture this home product she had sacrificed her agriculture. She must buy her food from abroad, and to do so she must sell her goods abroad.

But the struggle for commercial supremacy had not yet really begun. England was without a rival. Her navies controlled the sea. Her armies and her insular position gave her peace at home. The world was hers to exploit. For nearly fifty years she dominated the European, American, and Indian trade, while the great wars then convulsing society were destroying possible competitive capital and straining consumption to its utmost. The pioneer of the industrial nations, she thus received such a start in the new race for wealth that it is only today the other nations have succeeded in overtaking her. In 1820 the volume of her trade (imports and exports) was 68,000,000 pounds. In 1899 it had increased to 815,000,000 pounds, —— an increase of 1200 per cent in the volume of trade.

For nearly one hundred years England has been producing surplus value. She has been producing far more than she consumes, and this excess has swelled the volume of her capital. This capital has been invested in her enterprises at home and abroad, and in her shipping. In 1898 the Stock Exchange estimated British capital invested abroad at 1,900,000,000 pounds. But hand in hand with her foreign investments have grown her adverse balances of trade. For the ten years ending with 1868, her average yearly adverse balance was 52,000,000 pounds; ending with 1878, 81,000,000 pounds; ending with 1888, 101,000,000 pounds; and ending with 1898, 133,000,000 pounds. In the single year of 1897 it reached the portentous sum of 157,000,000 pounds.

But England's adverse balances of trade in themselves are nothing at which to be frightened. Hitherto they have been paid from out the earnings of her shipping and the interest on her foreign investments. But what does cause anxiety, however, is that, relative to the trade development of other countries, her export trade is falling off, without a corresponding diminution of her imports, and that her securities and foreign holdings do not seem able to stand the added strain. These she is being forced to sell in order to pull even. As the London Times gloomily remarks, "We are entering the twentieth century on the down grade, after a prolonged period of

The War of the Classes

business activity, high wages, high profits, and overflowing revenue." In other words, the mighty grasp England held over the resources and capital of the world is being relaxed. The control of its commerce and banking is slipping through her fingers. The sale of her foreign holdings advertises the fact that other nations are capable of buying them, and, further, that these other nations are busily producing surplus value.

The movement has become general. Today, passing from country to country, an ever-increasing tide of capital is welling up. Production is doubling and quadrupling upon itself. It used to be that the impoverished or undeveloped nations turned to England when it came to borrowing, but now Germany is competing keenly with her in this matter. France is not averse to lending great sums to Russia, and Austria-Hungary has capital and to spare for foreign holdings.

Nor has the United States failed to pass from the side of the debtor to that of the creditor nations. She, too, has become wise in the way of producing surplus value. She has been successful in her efforts to secure economic emancipation. Possessing but 5 per cent of the world's population and producing 32 per cent of the world's food supply, she has been looked upon as the world's farmer; but now, amidst general consternation, she comes forward as the world's manufacturer. In 1888 her manufactured exports amounted to $130,300,087; in 1896, to $253,681,541; in 1897, to $279,652,721; in 1898, to $307,924,994; in 1899, to $338,667,794; and in 1900, to $432,000,000. Regarding her growing favorable balances of trade, it may be noted that not only are her imports not increasing, but they are actually falling off, while her exports in the last decade have increased 72.4 per cent. In ten years her imports from Europe have been reduced from $474,000,000 to $439,000,000; while in the same time her exports have increased from $682,000,000 to $1,111,000,000. Her balance of trade in her favor in 1895 was $75,000,000; in 1896, over $100,000,000; in 1897, nearly $300,000,000; in 1898, $615,000,000; in 1899, $530,000,000; and in 1900, $648,000,000.

In the matter of iron, the United States, which in 1840 had not dreamed of entering the field of international competition, in 1897, as much to her own surprise as any one else's, undersold the English in their own London market. In 1899 there was but one American locomotive in Great Britain; but, of the five hundred locomotives sold abroad by the United States in 1902, England bought more than any other country. Russia is operating a thousand of them on her

The Question of the Maximum

own roads today. In one instance the American manufacturers contracted to deliver a locomotive in four and one-half months for $9250, the English manufacturers requiring twenty-four months for delivery at $14,000. The Clyde shipbuilders recently placed orders for 150,000 tons of plates at a saving of $250,000, and the American steel going into the making of the new London subway is taken as a matter of course. American tools stand above competition the world over. Ready-made boots and shoes are beginning to flood Europe, — the same with machinery, bicycles, agricultural implements, and all kinds of manufactured goods. A correspondent from Hamburg, speaking of the invasion of American trade, says: "Incidentally, it may be remarked that the typewriting machine with which this article is written, as well as the thousands — nay, hundreds of thousands — of others that are in use throughout the world, were made in America; that it stands on an American table, in an office furnished with American desks, bookcases, and chairs, which cannot be made in Europe of equal quality, so practical and convenient, for a similar price."

In 1893 and 1894, because of the distrust of foreign capital, the United States was forced to buy back American securities held abroad; but in 1897 and 1898 she bought back American securities held abroad, not because she had to, but because she chose to. And not only has she bought back her own securities, but in the last eight years she has become a buyer of the securities of other countries. In the money markets of London, Paris, and Berlin she is a lender of money. Carrying the largest stock of gold in the world, the world, in moments of danger, when crises of international finance loom large, looks to her vast lending ability for safety.

Thus, in a few swift years, has the United States drawn up to the van where the great industrial nations are fighting for commercial and financial empire. The figures of the race, in which she passed England, are interesting:

Year	United States Exports	United Kingdom Exports
1875	$497,263,737	$1,087,497,000
1885	673,593,506	1,037,124,000
1895	807,742,415	1,100,452,000
1896	986,830,080	1,168,671,000
1897	1,079,834,296	1,139,882,000
1898	1,233,564,828	1,135,642,000
1899	1,253,466,000	1,287,971,000
1900	1,453,013,659	1,418,348,000

The War of the Classes

As Mr. Henry Demarest Lloyd has noted, "When the news reached Germany of the new steel trust in America, the stocks of the iron and steel mills listed on the Berlin Bourse fell." While Europe has been talking and dreaming of the greatness which was, the United States has been thinking and planning and doing for the greatness to be. Her captains of industry and kings of finance have toiled and sweated at organizing and consolidating production and transportation. But this has been merely the developmental stage, the tuning-up of the orchestra. With the twentieth century rises the curtain on the play, — a play which shall have much in it of comedy and a vast deal of tragedy, and which has been well named The Capitalistic Conquest of Europe by America. Nations do not die easily, and one of the first moves of Europe will be the erection of tariff walls. America, however, will fittingly reply, for already her manufacturers are establishing works in France and Germany. And when the German trade journals refused to accept American advertisements, they found their country flamingly bill-boarded in buccaneer American fashion.

M. Leroy-Beaulieu, the French economist, is passionately preaching a commercial combination of the whole Continent against the United States, — a commercial alliance which, he boldly declares, should become a political alliance. And in this he is not alone, finding ready sympathy and ardent support in Austria, Italy, and Germany. Lord Rosebery said, in a recent speech before the Wolverhampton Chamber of Commerce: "The Americans, with their vast and almost incalculable resources, their acuteness and enterprise, and their huge population, which will probably be 100,000,000 in twenty years, together with the plan they have adopted for putting accumulated wealth into great cooperative syndicates or trusts for the purpose of carrying on this great commercial warfare, are the most formidable . . . rivals to be feared."

The London Times says: "It is useless to disguise the fact that Great Britain is being outdistanced. The competition does not come from the glut caused by miscalculation as to the home demand. Our own steel-makers know better and are alarmed. The threatened competition in markets hitherto our own comes from efficiency in production such as never before has been seen." Even the British naval supremacy is in danger, continues the same paper, "for, if we lose our engineering supremacy, our naval supremacy will follow, unless held on sufferance by our successful rivals."

And the Edinburgh Evening News says, with editorial gloom:

The Question of the Maximum

"The iron and steel trades have gone from us. When the fictitious prosperity caused by the expenditure of our own Government and that of European nations on armaments ceases, half of the men employed in these industries will be turned into the streets. The outlook is appalling. What suffering will have to be endured before the workers realize that there is nothing left for them but emigration!"

That there must be a limit to the accumulation of capital is obvious. The downward course of the rate of interest, notwithstanding that many new employments have been made possible for capital, indicates how large is the increase of surplus value. This decline of the interest rate is in accord with Bohm-Bawerk's law of "diminishing returns." That is, when capital, like anything else, has become over-plentiful, less lucrative use can only be found for the excess. This excess, not being able to earn so much as when capital was less plentiful, competes for safe investments and forces down the interest rate on all capital. Mr. Charles A. Conant has well described the keenness of the scramble for safe investments, even at the prevailing low rates of interest. At the close of the war with Turkey, the Greek loan, guaranteed by Great Britain, France, and Russia, was floated with striking ease. Regardless of the small return, the amount offered at Paris, (41,000,000 francs), was subscribed for twenty-three times over. Great Britain, France, Germany, Holland, and the Scandinavian States, of recent years, have all engaged in converting their securities from 5 per cents to 4 per cents, from 4.5 per cents to 3.5 per cents, and the 3.5 per cents into 3 per cents.

Great Britain, France, Germany, and Austria-Hungary, according to the calculation taken in 1895 by the International Statistical Institute, hold forty-six billions of capital invested in negotiable securities alone. Yet Paris subscribed for her portion of the Greek loan twenty-three times over! In short, money is cheap. Andrew Carnegie and his brother bourgeois kings give away millions annually, but still the tide wells up. These vast accumulations have made possible "wild-catting," fraudulent combinations, fake enterprises, Hooleyism; but such stealings, great though they be, have little or no effect in reducing the volume. The time is past when startling inventions, or revolutions in the method of production, can break up the growing congestion; yet this saved capital demands an outlet, somewhere, somehow.

When a great nation has equipped itself to produce far more

53

than it can, under the present division of the product, consume, it seeks other markets for its surplus products. When a second nation finds itself similarly circumstanced, competition for these other markets naturally follows. With the advent of a third, a fourth, a fifth, and of divers other nations, the question of the disposal of surplus products grows serious. And with each of these nations possessing, over and beyond its active capital, great and growing masses of idle capital, and when the very foreign markets for which they are competing are beginning to produce similar wares for themselves, the question passes the serious stage and becomes critical.

Never has the struggle for foreign markets been sharper than at the present. They are the one great outlet for congested accumulations. Predatory capital wanders the world over, seeking where it may establish itself. This urgent need for foreign markets is forcing upon the world-stage an era of great colonial empire. But this does not stand, as in the past, for the subjugation of peoples and countries for the sake of gaining their products, but for the privilege of selling them products. The theory once was, that the colony owed its existence and prosperity to the mother country; but today it is the mother country that owes its existence and prosperity to the colony. And in the future, when that supporting colony becomes wise in the way of producing surplus value and sends its goods back to sell to the mother country, what then? Then the world will have been exploited, and capitalistic production will have attained its maximum development.

Foreign markets and undeveloped countries largely retard that moment. The favored portions of the earth's surface are already occupied, though the resources of many are yet virgin. That they have not long since been wrested from the hands of the barbarous and decadent peoples who possess them is due, not to the military prowess of such peoples, but to the jealous vigilance of the industrial nations. The powers hold one another back. The Turk lives because the way is not yet clear to an amicable division of him among the powers. And the United States, supreme though she is, opposes the partition of China, and intervenes her huge bulk between the hungry nations and the mongrel Spanish republics. Capital stands in its own way, welling up and welling up against the inevitable moment when it shall burst all bonds and sweep resistlessly across such vast stretches as China and South America. And then there will be no more worlds to exploit, and capitalism will either fall back, crushed under its own weight, or a change of direction will take place which will mark a new era in history.

The Far East affords an illuminating spectacle. While the Western nations are crowding hungrily in, while the Partition of China is commingled with the clamor for the Spheres of Influence and the Open Door, other forces are none the less potently at work. Not only are the young Western peoples pressing the older ones to the wall, but the East itself is beginning to awake. American trade is advancing, and British trade is losing ground, while Japan, China, and India are taking a hand in the game themselves.

In 1893, 100,000 pieces of American drills were imported into China; in 1897, 349,000. In 1893, 252,000 pieces of American sheetings were imported against 71,000 British; but in 1897, 566,000 pieces of American sheetings were imported against only 10,000 British. The cotton goods and yarn trade (which forms 40 per cent of the whole trade with China) shows a remarkable advance on the part of the United States. During the last ten years America has increased her importation of plain goods by 121 per cent in quantity and 59.5 per cent in value, while that of England and India combined has decreased 13.75 per cent in quantity and 8 per cent in value. Lord Charles Beresford, from whose "Break-up of China" these figures are taken, states that English yarn has receded and Indian yarn advanced to the front. In 1897, 140,000 piculs of Indian yarn were imported, 18,000 of Japanese, 4500 of Shanghai-manufactured, and 700 of English.

Japan, who but yesterday emerged from the mediaeval rule of the Shogunate and seized in one fell swoop the scientific knowledge and culture of the Occident, is already today showing what wisdom she has acquired in the production of surplus value, and is preparing herself that she may tomorrow play the part to Asia that England did to Europe one hundred years ago. That the difference in the world's affairs wrought by those one hundred years will prevent her succeeding is manifest; but it is equally manifest that they cannot prevent her playing a leading part in the industrial drama which has commenced on the Eastern stage. Her imports into the port of Newchang in 1891 amounted to but 22,000 taels; but in 1897 they had increased to 280,000 taels. In manufactured goods, from matches, watches, and clocks to the rolling stock of railways, she has already given stiff shocks to her competitors in the Asiatic markets; and this while she is virtually yet in the equipment stage of production. Erelong she, too, will be furnishing her share to the growing mass of the world's capital.

As regards Great Britain, the giant trader who has so long overshadowed Asiatic commerce, Lord Charles Beresford says: "But competition is telling adversely; the energy of the British merchant is being equalled by other nationals... The competition of the Chinese and the introduction of steam into the country are also combining to produce changed conditions in China." But far more ominous is the plaintive note he sounds when he says: "New industries must be opened up, and I would especially direct the attention of the Chambers of Commerce (British) to ... the fact that the more the native competes with the British manufacturer in certain classes of trade, the more machinery he will need, and the orders for such machinery will come to this country if our machinery manufacturers are enterprising enough."

The Orient is beginning to show what an important factor it will become, under Western supervision, in the creation of surplus value. Even before the barriers which restrain Western capital are removed, the East will be in a fair way toward being exploited. An analysis of Lord Beresford's message to the Chambers of Commerce discloses, first, that the East is beginning to manufacture for itself; and, second, that there is a promise of keen competition in the West for the privilege of selling the required machinery. The inexorable query arises: *what is the west to do when it has furnished this machinery?* And when not only the East, but all the now undeveloped countries, confront, with surplus products in their hands, the old industrial nations, capitalistic production will have attained its maximum development.

But before that time must intervene a period which bids one pause for breath. A new romance, like unto none in all the past, the economic romance, will be born. For the dazzling prize of world-empire will the nations of the earth go up in harness. Powers will rise and fall, and mighty coalitions shape and dissolve in the swift whirl of events. Vassal nations and subject territories will be bandied back and forth like so many articles of trade. And with the inevitable displacement of economic centres, it is fair to presume that populations will shift to and fro, as they once did from the South to the North of England on the rise of the factory towns, or from the Old World to the New. Colossal enterprises will be projected and carried through, and combinations of capital and federations of labor be effected on a cyclopean scale. Concentration

The Question of the Maximum

and organization will be perfected in ways hitherto undreamed. The nation which would keep its head above the tide must accurately adjust supply to demand, and eliminate waste to the last least particle. Standards of living will most likely descend for millions of people. With the increase of capital, the competition for safe investments, and the consequent fall of the interest rate, the principal which today earns a comfortable income would not then support a bare existence. Saving toward old age would cease among the working classes. And as the merchant cities of Italy crashed when trade slipped from their hands on the discovery of the new route to the Indies by way of the Cape of Good Hope, so will there come times of trembling for such nations as have failed to grasp the prize of world-empire. In that given direction they will have attained their maximum development, before the whole world, in the same direction, has attained its. There will no longer be room for them. But if they can survive the shock of being flung out of the world's industrial orbit, a change in direction may then be easily effected. That the decadent and barbarous peoples will be crushed is a fair presumption; likewise that the stronger breeds will survive, entering upon the transition stage to which all the world must ultimately come.

This change of direction must be either toward industrial oligarchies or socialism. Either the functions of private corporations will increase till they absorb the central government, or the functions of government will increase till it absorbs the corporations. Much may be said on the chance of the oligarchy. Should an old manufacturing nation lose its foreign trade, it is safe to predict that a strong effort would be made to build a socialistic government, but it does not follow that this effort would be successful. With the moneyed class controlling the State and its revenues and all the means of subsistence, and guarding its own interests with jealous care, it is not at all impossible that a strong curb could be put upon the masses till the crisis were past. It has been done before. There is no reason why it should not be done again. At the close of the last century, such a movement was crushed by its own folly and immaturity. In 1871 the soldiers of the economic rulers stamped out, root and branch, a whole generation of militant socialists.

Once the crisis were past, the ruling class, still holding the curb in order to make itself more secure, would proceed to readjust things and to balance consumption with production. Having a monopoly of the safe investments, the great masses of unremunerative capital would be directed, not to the production of more surplus value, but to the making of permanent improvements, which would give employment to the people, and make them content with the new order of things. Highways, parks, public buildings, monuments, could be builded; nor would it be out of place to give better factories and homes to the workers. Such in itself would be socialistic, save that it would be done by the oligarchs, a class apart. With the interest rate down to zero, and no field for the investment of sporadic capital, savings among the people would utterly cease, and old-age pensions be granted as a matter of course. It is also a logical necessity of such a system that, when the population began to press against the means of subsistence, (expansion being impossible), the birth rate of the lower classes would be lessened. Whether by their own initiative, or by the interference of the rulers, it would have to be done, and it would be done. In other words, the oligarchy would mean the capitalization of labor and the enslavement of the whole population. But it would be a fairer, juster form of slavery than any the world has yet seen. The per capita wage and consumption would be increased, and, with a stringent control of the birth rate, there is no reason why such a country should not be so ruled through many generations.

On the other hand, as the capitalistic exploitation of the planet approaches its maximum, and countries are crowded out of the field of foreign exchanges, there is a large likelihood that their change in direction will be toward socialism. Were the theory of collective ownership and operation then to arise for the first time, such a movement would stand small chance of success. But such is not the case. The doctrine of socialism has flourished and grown throughout the nineteenth century; its tenets have been preached wherever the interests of labor and capital have clashed; and it has received exemplification time and again by the State's assumption of functions which had always belonged solely to the individual.

When capitalistic production has attained its maximum development, it must confront a dividing of the ways; and the strength of capital on the one hand, and the education and wisdom of the workers on the other, will determine which path society is to travel. It is possible, considering the inertia of the masses, that the whole world might in time come to be dominated by a group of industrial oligarchies, or by one great oligarchy, but it is not probable. That sporadic oligarchies may flourish for definite periods of time is highly possible; that they may continue to do so is as highly improbable. The procession of the ages has marked not only the

The Question of the Maximum

rise of man, but the rise of the common man. From the chattel slave, or the serf chained to the soil, to the highest seats in modern society, he has risen, rung by rung, amid the crumbling of the divine right of kings and the crash of falling sceptres. That he has done this, only in the end to pass into the perpetual slavery of the industrial oligarch, is something at which his whole past cries in protest. The common man is worthy of a better future, or else he is not worthy of his past.

Note.

—— The above article was written as long ago as 1898. The only alteration has been the bringing up to 1900 of a few of its statistics. As a commercial venture of an author, it has an interesting history. It was promptly accepted by one of the leading magazines and paid for. The editor confessed that it was "one of those articles one could not possibly let go of after it was once in his possession." Publication was voluntarily promised to be immediate. Then the editor became afraid of its too radical nature, forfeited the sum paid for it, and did not publish it. Nor, offered far and wide, could any other editor of bourgeois periodicals be found who was rash enough to publish it. Thus, for the first time, after seven years, it appears in print.

A Review

TWO remarkable books are Ghent's "Our Benevolent Feudalism"* and Brooks's "The Social Unrest."** In these two books the opposite sides of the labor problem are expounded, each writer devoting himself with apprehension to the side he fears and views with disfavor. It would appear that they have set themselves the task of collating, as a warning, the phenomena of two counter social forces. Mr. Ghent, who is sympathetic with the socialist movement, follows with cynic fear every aggressive act of the capitalist class. Mr. Brooks, who yearns for the perpetuation of the capitalist system as long as possible, follows with grave dismay each aggressive act of the labor and socialist organizations. Mr. Ghent traces the emasculation of labor by capital, and Mr. Brooks traces the emasculation of independent competing capital by labor. In short, each marshals the facts of a side in the two sides which go to make a struggle so great that even the French Revolution is insignificant beside it; for this later struggle, for the first time in the history of struggles, is not confined to any particular portion of the globe, but involves the whole of it.

Starting on the assumption that society is at present in a state of flux, Mr. Ghent sees it rapidly crystallizing into a status which can best be described as something in the nature of a benevolent feudalism. He laughs to scorn any immediate realization of the Marxian dream, while Tolstoyan utopias and Kropotkinian communistic unions of shop and farm are too wild to merit consideration. The coming status which Mr. Ghent depicts is a class domination by the capitalists. Labor will take its definite place as a dependent class, living in a condition of machine servitude fairly analogous to the land servitude of the Middle Ages. That is to say, labor will be bound to the machine, though less harshly, in fashion somewhat similar to that in which the earlier serf was bound to the soil. As he says, "Bondage to the land was the basis of villeinage in the old regime; bondage to the job will be the basis of villeinage in the new."

At the top of the new society will tower the magnate, the new

*"Our Benevolent Feudalism." By W. J. Ghent. The Macmillan Company.

**"The Social Unrest." By John Graham Brooks. The Macmillan Company.

A Review

feudal baron; at the bottom will be found the wastrels and the inefficients. The new society he grades as follows:

"I. The barons, graded on the basis of possessions.

"III. The court agents and retainers. (This class will include the editors of 'respectable' and 'safe' newspapers, the pastors of 'conservative' and 'wealthy' churches, the professors and teachers in endowed colleges and schools, lawyers generally, and most judges and politicians).

"III. The workers in pure and applied science, artists, and physicians.

"IV. The entrepreneurs, the managers of the great industries, transformed into a salaried class.

"V. The foremen and superintendents. This class has heretofore been recruited largely from the skilled workers, but with the growth of technical education in schools and colleges, and the development of fixed caste, it is likely to become entirely differentiated.

"IV. The villeins of the cities and towns, more or less regularly employed, who do skilled work and are partially protected by organization.

"VII. The villeins of the cities and towns who do unskilled work and are unprotected by organization. They will comprise the laborers, domestics, and clerks.

"VIII. The villeins of the manorial estates, of the great farms, the mines, and the forests.

"IX. The small-unit farmers (land-owning), the petty tradesmen, and manufacturers.

"X. The subtenants of the manorial estates and great farms (corresponding to the class of 'free tenants' in the old Feudalism).

"XI. The cotters.

"XII. The tramps, the occasionally employed, the unemployed — the wastrels of the city and country."

"The new Feudalism, like most autocracies, will foster not only the arts, but also certain kinds of learning — particularly the kinds which are unlikely to disturb the minds of the multitude. A future Marsh, or Cope, or Le Comte will be liberally patronized and left free to discover what he will; and so, too, an Edison or a Marconi. Only they must not meddle with anything relating to social science."

61

The War of the Classes

It must be confessed that Mr. Ghent's arguments are cunningly contrived and arrayed. They must be read to be appreciated. As an example of his style, which at the same time generalizes a portion of his argument, the following may well be given:

"The new Feudalism will be but an orderly outgrowth of present tendencies and conditions. All societies evolve naturally out of their predecessors. In sociology, as in biology, there is no cell without a parent cell. The society of each generation develops a multitude of spontaneous and acquired variations, and out of these, by a blending process of natural and conscious selection, the succeeding society is evolved. The new order will differ in no important respects from the present, except in the completer development of its more salient features. The visitor from another planet who had known the old and should see the new would note but few changes. Alter et Idem — another yet the same — he would say. From magnate to baron, from workman to villein, from publicist to court agent and retainer, will be changes of state and function so slight as to elude all but the keenest eyes."

And in conclusion, to show how benevolent and beautiful this new feudalism of ours will be, Mr. Ghent says: "Peace and stability it will maintain at all hazards; and the mass, remembering the chaos, the turmoil, the insecurity of the past, will bless its reign. . . . Efficiency — the faculty of getting things — is at last rewarded as it should be, for the efficient have inherited the earth and its fulness. The lowly, whose happiness is greater and whose welfare is more thoroughly conserved when governed than when governing, as a twentieth-century philosopher said of them, are settled and happy in the state which reason and experience teach is their God-appointed lot. They are comfortable too; and if the patriarchal ideal of a vine and fig tree for each is not yet attained, at least each has his rented patch in the country or his rented cell in a city building. Bread and the circus are freely given to the deserving, and as for the undeserving, they are merely reaping the rewards of their contumacy and pride. Order reigns, each has his justly appointed share, and the state rests, in security, 'lapt in universal law.'"

Mr. Brooks, on the other hand, sees rising and dissolving and rising again in the social flux the ominous forms of a new society which is the direct antithesis of a benevolent feudalism. He trembles at the rash intrepidity of the capitalists who fight the labor unions, for by such rashness he greatly fears that labor will be

A Review

driven to express its aims and strength in political terms, which terms will inevitably be socialistic terms.

To keep down the rising tide of socialism, he preaches greater meekness and benevolence to the capitalists. No longer may they claim the right to run their own business, to beat down the laborer's standard of living for the sake of increased profits, to dictate terms of employment to individual workers, to wax righteously indignant when organized labor takes a hand in their business. No longer may the capitalist say "my" business, or even think "my" business; he must say "our" business, and think "our" business as well, accepting labor as a partner whose voice must be heard. And if the capitalists do not become more meek and benevolent in their dealings with labor, labor will be antagonized and will proceed to wreak terrible political vengeance, and the present social flux will harden into a status of socialism.

Mr. Brooks dreams of a society at which Mr. Ghent sneers as "a slightly modified individualism, wherein each unit secures the just reward of his capacity and service." To attain this happy state, Mr. Brooks imposes circumspection upon the capitalists in their relations with labor. "If the socialistic spirit is to be held in abeyance in this country, businesses of this character (anthracite coal mining) must be handled with extraordinary caution." Which is to say, that to withstand the advance of socialism, a great and greater measure of Mr. Ghent's *benevolence* will be required.

Again and again, Mr. Brooks reiterates the danger he sees in harshly treating labor. "It is not probable that employers can destroy unionism in the United States. Adroit and desperate attempts will, however, be made, if we mean by unionism the undisciplined and aggressive fact of vigorous and determined organizations. If capital should prove too strong in this struggle, the result is easy to predict. The employers have only to convince organized labor that it cannot hold its own against the capitalist manager, and the whole energy that now goes to the union will turn to an aggressive political socialism. It will not be the harmless sympathy with increased city and state functions which trade unions already feel; it will become a turbulent political force bent upon using every weapon of taxation against the rich."

"The most concrete impulse that now favors socialism in this country is the insane purpose to deprive labor organizations of the full and complete rights that go with federated unionism."

"That which teaches a union that it cannot succeed as a union

The War of the Classes

turns it toward socialism. In long strikes in towns like Marlboro and Brookfield strong unions are defeated. Hundreds of men leave these towns for shoe-centres like Brockton, where they are now voting the socialist ticket. The socialist mayor of this city tells me, 'The men who come to us now from towns where they have been thoroughly whipped in a strike are among our most active working socialists.' The bitterness engendered by this sense of defeat is turned to politics, as it will throughout the whole country, if organization of labor is deprived of its rights."

"This enmity of capital to the trade union is watched with glee by every intelligent socialist in our midst. Every union that is beaten or discouraged in its struggle is ripening fruit for socialism."

"The real peril which we now face is the threat of a class conflict. If capitalism insists upon the policy of outraging the saving aspiration of the American workman to raise his standard of comfort and leisure, every element of class conflict will strengthen among us."

"We have only to humiliate what is best in the trade union, and then every worst feature of socialism is fastened upon us."

This strong tendency in the ranks of the workers toward socialism is what Mr. Brooks characterizes the "social unrest"; and he hopes to see the Republican, the Cleveland Democrat, and the conservative and large property interests "band together against this common foe," which is socialism. And he is not above feeling grave and well-contained satisfaction wherever the socialist doctrinaire has been contradicted by men attempting to practise cooperation in the midst of the competitive system, as in Belgium.

Nevertheless, he catches fleeting glimpses of an extreme and tyrannically benevolent feudalism very like to Mr. Ghent's, as witness the following:

"I asked one of the largest employers of labor in the South if he feared the coming of the trade union. 'No,' he said, 'it is one good result of race prejudice, that the negro will enable us in the long run to weaken the trade union so that it cannot harm us. We can keep wages down with the negro and we can prevent too much organization.'

"It is in this spirit that the lower standards are to be used. If this purpose should succeed, it has but one issue, — the immense strengthening of a plutocratic administration at the top, served by an army of high-salaried helpers, with an elite of skilled and well-paid workmen, but all resting on what would essentially be a serf class of

A Review

low-paid labor and this mass kept in order by an increased use of military force."

In brief summary of these two notable books, it may be said that Mr. Ghent is alarmed, (though he does not flatly say so), at the too great social restfulness in the community, which is permitting the capitalists to form the new society to their liking; and that Mr. Brooks is alarmed, (and he flatly says so), at the social unrest which threatens the modified individualism into which he would like to see society evolve. Mr. Ghent beholds the capitalist class rising to dominate the state and the working class; Mr. Brooks beholds the working class rising to dominate the state and the capitalist class. One fears the paternalism of a class; the other, the tyranny of the mass.

Wanted:
A NEW LAND OF DEVELOPMENT

EVOLUTION is no longer a mere tentative hypothesis. One by one, step by step, each division and subdivision of science has contributed its evidence, until now the case is complete and the verdict rendered. While there is still discussion as to the method of evolution, none the less, as a process sufficient to explain all biological phenomena, all differentiations of life into widely diverse species, families, and even kingdoms, evolution is flatly accepted. Likewise has been accepted its law of development: *that, in the struggle for existence, the strong and fit and the progeny of the strong and fit have a better opportunity for survival than the weak and less fit and the progeny of the weak and less fit.*

It is in the struggle of the species with other species and against all other hostile forces in the environment, that this law operates; also in the struggle between the individuals of the same species. In this struggle, which is for food and shelter, the weak individuals must obviously win less food and shelter than the strong. Because of this, their hold on life relaxes and they are eliminated. And for the same reason that they may not win for themselves adequate food and shelter, the weak cannot give to their progeny the chance for survival that the strong give. And thus, since the weak are prone to beget weakness, the species is constantly purged of its inefficient members.

Because of this, a premium is placed upon strength, and so long as the struggle for food and shelter obtains, just so long will the average strength of each generation increase. On the other hand, should conditions so change that all, and the progeny of all, the weak as well as the strong, have an equal chance for survival, then, at once, the average strength of each generation will begin to diminish. Never yet, however, in animal life, has there been such a state of affairs. Natural selection has always obtained. The strong and their progeny, at the expense of the weak, have always survived. This law of development has operated down all the past upon all life; it so operates today, and it is not rash to say that it will continue to operate in the future — at least upon all life existing in a state of nature.

Man, preeminent though he is in the animal kingdom, capable

66

Wanted: A New Land of Development

of reacting upon and making suitable an unsuitable environment, nevertheless remains the creature of this same law of development. The social selection to which he is subject is merely another form of natural selection. True, within certain narrow limits he modifies the struggle for existence and renders less precarious the tenure of life for the weak. The extremely weak, diseased, and inefficient are housed in hospitals and asylums. The strength of the viciously strong, when inimical to society, is tempered by penal institutions and by the gallows. The short-sighted are provided with spectacles, and the sickly (when they can pay for it) with sanitariums. Pestilential marshes are drained, plagues are checked, and disasters averted. Yet, for all that, the strong and the progeny of the strong survive, and the weak are crushed out. The men strong of brain are masters as of yore. They dominate society and gather to themselves the wealth of society. With this wealth they maintain themselves and equip their progeny for the struggle. They build their homes in healthful places, purchase the best fruits, meats, and vegetables the market affords, and buy themselves the ministrations of the most brilliant and learned of the professional classes. The weak man, as of yore, is the servant, the doer of things at the master's call. The weaker and less efficient he is, the poorer is his reward. The weakest work for a living wage, (when they can get work), live in unsanitary slums, on vile and insufficient food, at the lowest depths of human degradation. Their grasp on life is indeed precarious, their mortality excessive, their infant death-rate appalling.

That some should be born to preferment and others to ignominy in order that the race may progress, is cruel and sad; but none the less they are so born. The weeding out of human souls, some for fatness and smiles, some for leanness and tears, is surely a heartless selective process — as heartless as it is natural. And the human family, for all its wonderful record of adventure and achievement, has not yet succeeded in avoiding this process. That it is incapable of doing this is not to be hazarded. Not only is it capable, but the whole trend of society is in that direction. All the social forces are driving man on to a time when the old selective law will be annulled. There is no escaping it, save by the intervention of catastrophes and cataclysms quite unthinkable. It is inexorable. It is inexorable because the common man demands it. The twentieth century, the common man says, is his day; the common man's day, or, rather, the dawning of the common man's day.

Nor can it be denied. The evidence is with him. The previous

67

The War of the Classes

centuries, and more notably the nineteenth, have marked the rise of the common man. From chattel slavery to serfdom, and from serfdom to what he bitterly terms "wage slavery," he has risen. Never was he so strong as he is today, and never so menacing. He does the work of the world, and he is beginning to know it. The world cannot get along without him, and this also he is beginning to know. All the human knowledge of the past, all the scientific discovery, governmental experiment, and invention of machinery, have tended to his advancement. His standard of living is higher. His common school education would shame princes ten centuries past. His civil and religious liberty makes him a free man, and his ballot the peer of his betters. And all this has tended to make him conscious, conscious of himself, conscious of his class. He looks about him and questions that ancient law of development. It is cruel and wrong, he is beginning to declare. It is an anachronism. Let it be abolished. Why should there be one empty belly in all the world, when the work of ten men can feed a hundred? What if my brother be not so strong as I? He has not sinned. Wherefore should he hunger — he and his sinless little ones? Away with the old law. There is food and shelter for all, therefore let all receive food and shelter.

As fast as labor has become conscious it has organized. The ambition of these class-conscious men is that the movement shall become general, that all labor shall become conscious of itself and its class interests. And the day that witnesses the solidarity of labor, they triumphantly affirm, will be a day when labor dominates the world. This growing consciousness has led to the organization of two movements, both separate and distinct, but both converging toward a common goal — one, the labor movement, known as Trade Unionism; the other, the political movement, known as Socialism. Both are grim and silent forces, unheralded and virtually unknown to the general public save in moments of stress. The sleeping labor giant receives little notice from the capitalistic press, and when he stirs uneasily, a column of surprise, indignation, and horror suffices.

It is only now and then, after long periods of silence, that the labor movement puts in its claim for notice. All is quiet. The kind old world spins on, and the bourgeois masters clip their coupons in smug complacency. But the grim and silent forces are at work.

Suddenly, like a clap of thunder from a clear sky, comes a disruption of industry. From ocean to ocean the wheels of a great chain of railroads cease to run. A quarter of a million miners throw down pick and shovel and outrage the sun with their pale, bleached faces. The street railways of a swarming metropolis stand idle, or the rumble of machinery in vast manufactories dies away to silence. There is alarm and panic. Arson and homicide stalk forth. There is a cry in the night, and quick anger and sudden death. Peaceful cities are affrighted by the crack of rifles and the snarl of machine-guns, and the hearts of the shuddering are shaken by the roar of dynamite. There is hurrying and skurrying. The wires are kept hot between the centre of government and the seat of trouble. The chiefs of state ponder gravely and advise, and governors of states implore. There is assembling of militia and massing of troops, and the streets resound to the tramp of armed men. There are separate and joint conferences between the captains of industry and the captains of labor. And then, finally, all is quiet again, and the memory of it is like the memory of a bad dream.

But these strikes become olympiads, things to date from; and common on the lips of men become such phrases as "The Great Dock Strike," "The Great Coal Strike," "The Great Railroad Strike." Never before did labor do these things. After the Great Plague in England, labor, finding itself in demand and innocently obeying the economic law, asked higher wages. But the masters set a maximum wage, restrained workingmen from moving about from place to place, refused to tolerate idlers, and by most barbarous legal methods punished those who disobeyed. But labor is accorded greater respect today. Such a policy, put into effect in this the first decade of the twentieth century, would sweep the masters from their seats in one mighty crash. And the masters know it and are respectful.

A fair instance of the growing solidarity of labor is afforded by an unimportant recent strike in San Francisco. The restaurant cooks and waiters were completely unorganized, working at any and all hours for whatever wages they could get. A representative of the American Federation of Labor went among them and organized them. Within a few weeks nearly two thousand men were enrolled, and they had five thousand dollars on deposit. Then they put in their demand for increased wages and shorter hours. Forthwith their employers organized. The demand was denied, and the Cooks' and Waiters' Union walked out.

All organized employers stood back of the restaurant owners, in sympathy with them and willing to aid them if they dared. And at the back of the Cooks' and Waiters' Union stood the organized labor of the city, 40,000 strong. If a business man was caught patronizing

The War of the Classes

an "unfair" restaurant, he was boycotted; if a union man was caught, he was fined heavily by his union or expelled. The oyster companies and the slaughter houses made an attempt to refuse to sell oysters and meat to union restaurants. The Butchers and Meat Cutters, and the Teamsters, in retaliation, refused to work for or to deliver to non-union restaurants. Upon this the oyster companies and slaughter houses acknowledged themselves beaten and peace reigned. But the Restaurant Bakers in non-union places were ordered out, and the Bakery Wagon Drivers declined to deliver to unfair houses.

Every American Federation of Labor union in the city was prepared to strike, and waited only the word. And behind all, a handful of men, known as the Labor Council, directed the fight. One by one, blow upon blow, they were able if they deemed it necessary to call out the unions — the Laundry Workers, who do the washing; the Hackmen, who haul men to and from restaurants; the Butchers, Meat Cutters, and Teamsters; and the Milkers, Milk Drivers, and Chicken Pickers; and after that, in pure sympathy, the Retail Clerks, the Horse Shoers, the Gas and Electrical Fixture Hangers, the Metal Roofers, the Blacksmiths, the Blacksmiths' Helpers, the Stablemen, the Machinists, the Brewers, the Coast Seamen, the Varnishers and Polishers, the Confectioners, the Upholsterers, the Paper Hangers and Fresco Painters, the Drug Clerks, the Fitters and Helpers, the Metal Workers, the Boiler Makers and Iron Ship Builders, the Assistant Undertakers, the Carriage and Wagon Workers, and so on down the lengthy list of organizations.

For, over all these trades, over all these thousands of men, is the Labor Council. When it speaks its voice is heard, and when it orders it is obeyed. But it, in turn, is dominated by the National Labor Council, with which it is constantly in touch. In this wholly unimportant little local strike it is of interest to note the stands taken by the different sides. The legal representative and official mouthpiece of the Employers' Association said: "This organization is formed for defensive purposes, and it may be driven to take offensive steps, and if so, will be strong enough to follow them up. Labor cannot be allowed to dictate to capital and say how business shall be conducted. There is no objection to the formation of unions and trades councils, but membership must not be compulsory. It is repugnant to the American idea of liberty and cannot be tolerated."

On the other hand, the president of the Team Drivers' Union

Wanted: A New Land of Development

said: "The employers of labor in this city are generally against the trade-union movement and there seems to be a concerted effort on their part to check the progress of organized labor. Such action as has been taken by them in sympathy with the present labor troubles may, if continued, lead to a serious conflict, the outcome of which might be most calamitous for the business and industrial interests of San Francisco."

And the secretary of the United Brewery Workmen: "I regard a sympathetic strike as the last weapon which organized labor should use in its defence. When, however, associations of employers band together to defeat organized labor, or one of its branches, then we should not and will not hesitate ourselves to employ the same instrument in retaliation."

Thus, in a little corner of the world, is exemplified the growing solidarity of labor. The organization of labor has not only kept pace with the organization of industry, but it has gained upon it. In one winter, in the anthracite coal region, $160,000,000 in mines and $600,000,000 in transportation and distribution consolidated its ownership and control. And at once, arrayed as solidly on the other side, were the 150,000 anthracite miners. The bituminous mines, however, were not consolidated; yet the 250,000 men employed therein were already combined. And not only that, but they were also combined with the anthracite miners, these 400,000 men being under the control and direction of one supreme labor council. And in this and the other great councils are to be found captains of labor of splendid abilities, who, in understanding of economic and industrial conditions, are undeniably the equals of their opponents, the captains of industry.

The United States is honeycombed with labor organizations. And the big federations which these go to compose aggregate millions of members, and in their various branches handle millions of dollars yearly. And not only this; for the international brotherhoods and unions are forming, and moneys for the aid of strikers pass back and forth across the seas. The Machinists, in their demand for a nine-hour day, affected 500,000 men in the United States, Mexico, and Canada. In England the membership of working-class organizations is approximated by Keir Hardie at 2,500,000, with reserve funds of $18,000,000. There the cooperative movement has a membership of 1,500,000, and every year turns over in distribution more than $100,000,000. In France, one-eighth of the whole working class is unionized. In Belgium the unions are very rich and

71

powerful, and so able to defy the masters that many of the smaller manufacturers, unable to resist, "are removing their works to other countries where the workmen's organizations are not so potential." And in all other countries, according to the stage of their economic and political development, like figures obtain. And Europe, today, confesses that her greatest social problem is the labor problem, and that it is the one most closely engrossing the attention of her statesmen.

The organization of labor is one of the chief acknowledged factors in the retrogression of British trade. The workers have become class conscious as never before. The wrong of one is the wrong of all. They have come to realize, in a short-sighted way, that their masters' interests are not their interests. The harder they work, they believe, the more wealth they create for their masters. Further, the more work they do in one day, the fewer men will be needed to do the work. So the unions place a day's stint upon their members, beyond which they are not permitted to go. In "A Study of Trade Unionism," by Benjamin Taylor in the "Nineteenth Century" of April, 1898, are furnished some interesting corroborations. The facts here set forth were collected by the Executive Board of the Employers' Federation, the documentary proofs of which are in the hands of the secretaries. In a certain firm the union workmen made eight ammunition boxes a day. Nor could they be persuaded into making more. A young Swiss, who could not speak English, was set to work, and in the first day he made fifty boxes. In the same firm the skilled union hands filed up the outside handles of one machine-gun a day. That was their stint. No one was known ever to do more. A non-union filer came into the shop and did twelve a day. A Manchester firm found that to plane a large bed-casting took union workmen one hundred and ninety hours, and non-union workmen one hundred and thirty-five hours. In another instance a man, resigning from his union, day by day did double the amount of work he had done formerly. And to cap it all, an English gentleman, going out to look at a wall being put up for him by union bricklayers, found one of their number with his right arm strapped to his body, doing all the work with his left arm -forsooth, because he was such an energetic fellow that otherwise he would involuntarily lay more bricks than his union permitted.

All England resounds to the cry, "Wake up, England!" But the sulky giant is not stirred. "Let England's trade go to pot," he says; "what have I to lose?" And England is powerless. The capacity of

Wanted: A New Land of Development

her workmen is represented by 1, in comparison with the 2.25 capacity of the American workman. And because of the solidarity of labor and the destructiveness of strikes, British capitalists dare not even strive to emulate the enterprise of American capitalists. So England watches trade slipping through her fingers and wails unavailingly. As a correspondent writes: "The enormous power of the trade unions hangs, a sullen cloud, over the whole industrial world here, affecting men and masters alike."

The political movement known as Socialism is, perhaps, even less realized by the general public. The great strides it has taken and the portentous front it today exhibits are not comprehended; and, fastened though it is in every land, it is given little space by the capitalistic press. For all its plea and passion and warmth, it wells upward like a great, cold tidal wave, irresistible, inexorable, ingulfing present-day society level by level. By its own preachment it is inexorable. Just as societies have sprung into existence, fulfilled their function, and passed away, it claims, just as surely is present society hastening on to its dissolution. This is a transition period — and destined to be a very short one. Barely a century old, capitalism is ripening so rapidly that it can never live to see a second birthday. There is no hope for it, the Socialists say. It is doomed.

The cardinal tenet of Socialism is that forbidding doctrine, the materialistic conception of history. Men are not the masters of their souls. They are the puppets of great, blind forces. The lives they live and the deaths they die are compulsory. All social codes are but the reflexes of existing economic conditions, plus certain survivals of past economic conditions. The institutions men build they are compelled to build. Economic laws determine at any given time what these institutions shall be, how long they shall operate, and by what they shall be replaced. And so, through the economic process, the Socialist preaches the ripening of the capitalistic society and the coming of the new cooperative society.

The second great tenet of Socialism, itself a phase of the materialistic conception of history, is the class struggle. In the social struggle for existence, men are forced into classes. "The history of all society thus far is the history of class strife." In existing society the capitalist class exploits the working class, the proletariat. The interests of the exploiter are not the interests of the exploited. "Profits are legitimate," says the one. "Profits are unpaid wages," replies the other, when he has become conscious of his class,

73

The War of the Classes

"therefore profits are robbery." The capitalist enforces his profits because he is the legal owner of all the means of production. He is the legal owner because he controls the political machinery of society. The Socialist sets to work to capture the political machinery, so that he may make illegal the capitalist's ownership of the means of production, and make legal his own ownership of the means of production. And it is this struggle, between these two classes, upon which the world has at last entered.

Scientific Socialism is very young. Only yesterday it was in swaddling clothes. But today it is a vigorous young giant, well braced to battle for what it wants, and knowing precisely what it wants. It holds its international conventions, where world-policies are formulated by the representatives of millions of Socialists. In little Belgium there are three-quarters of a million of men who work for the cause; in Germany, 3,000,000; Austria, between 1895 and 1897, raised her socialist vote from 90,000 to 750,000. France in 1871 had a whole generation of Socialists wiped out; yet in 1885 there were 30,000, and in 1898, 1,000,000.

Ere the last Spaniard had evacuated Cuba, Socialist groups were forming. And from far Japan, in these first days of the twentieth century, writes one Tomoyoshi Murai: "The interest of our people on Socialism has been greatly awakened these days, especially among our laboring people on one hand and young students' circle on the other, as much as we can draw an earnest and enthusiastic audience and fill our hall, which holds two thousand. . . . It is gratifying to say that we have a number of fine and well-trained public orators among our leaders of Socialism in Japan. The first speaker tonight is Mr. Kiyoshi Kawakami, editor of one of our city (Tokyo) dailies, a strong, independent, and decidedly socialistic paper, circulated far and wide. Mr. Kawakami is a scholar as well as a popular writer. He is going to speak tonight on the subject, 'The Essence of Socialism — the Fundamental Principles.' The next speaker is Professor Iso Abe, president of our association, whose subject of address is, 'Socialism and the Existing Social System.' The third speaker is Mr. Naoe Kinosita, the editor of another strong journal of the city. He speaks on the subject, 'How to Realize the Socialist Ideals and Plans.' Next is Mr. Shigeyoshi Sugiyama, a graduate of Hartford Theological Seminary and an advocate of Social Christianity, who is to speak on 'Socialism and Municipal Problems.' And the last speaker is the editor of the 'Labor World,' the foremost leader of the labor-union movement in our country,

Wanted: A New Land of Development

Mr. Sen Katayama, who speaks on the subject, 'The Outlook of Socialism in Europe and America.' These addresses are going to be published in book form and to be distributed among our people to enlighten their minds on the subject."

And in the struggle for the political machinery of society, Socialism is no longer confined to mere propaganda. Italy, Austria, Belgium, England, have Socialist members in their national bodies. Out of the one hundred and thirty-two members of the London County Council, ninety-one are denounced by the conservative element as Socialists. The Emperor of Germany grows anxious and angry at the increasing numbers which are returned to the Reichstag. In France, many of the large cities, such as Marseilles, are in the hands of the Socialists. A large body of them is in the Chamber of Deputies, and Millerand, Socialist, sits in the cabinet. Of him M. Leroy-Beaulieu says with horror: "M. Millerand is the open enemy of private property, private capital, the resolute advocate of the socialization of production . . . a constant incitement to violence . . . a collectivist, avowed and militant, taking part in the government, dominating the departments of commerce and industry, preparing all the laws and presiding at the passage of all measures which should be submitted to merchants and tradesmen."

In the United States there are already Socialist mayors of towns and members of State legislatures, a vast literature, and single Socialist papers with subscription lists running up into the hundreds of thousands. In 1896, 36,000 votes were cast for the Socialist candidate for President; in 1900, nearly 200,000; in 1904, 450,000. And the United States, young as it is, is ripening rapidly, and the Socialists claim, according to the materialistic conception of history, that the United States will be the first country in the world wherein the toilers will capture the political machinery and expropriate the bourgeoisie.

But the Socialist and labor movements have recently entered upon a new phase. There has been a remarkable change in attitude on both sides. For a long time the labor unions refrained from going in for political action. On the other hand, the Socialists claimed that without political action labor was powerless. And because of this there was much ill feeling between them, even open hostilities, and no concerted action. But now the Socialists grant that the labor movement has held up wages and decreased the hours of labor, and the labor unions find that political action is necessary. Today both

The War of the Classes

parties have drawn closely together in the common fight. In the United States this friendly feeling grows. The Socialist papers espouse the cause of labor, and the unions have opened their ears once more to the wiles of the Socialists. They are all leavened with Socialist workmen, "boring from within," and many of their leaders have already succumbed. In England, where class consciousness is more developed, the name "Unionism" has been replaced by "The New Unionism," the main object of which is "to capture existing social structures in the interests of the wage-earners." There the Socialist, the trade-union, and other working-class organizations are beginning to cooperate in securing the return of representatives to the House of Commons. And in France, where the city councils and mayors of Marseilles and Monteaules-Mines are Socialistic, thousands of francs of municipal money were voted for the aid of the unions in the recent great strikes.

For centuries the world has been preparing for the coming of the common man. And the period of preparation virtually past, labor, conscious of itself and its desires, has begun a definite movement toward solidarity. It believes the time is not far distant when the historian will speak not only of the dark ages of feudalism, but of the dark ages of capitalism. And labor sincerely believes itself justified in this by the terrible indictment it brings against capitalistic society. In the face of its enormous wealth, capitalistic society forfeits its right to existence when it permits widespread, bestial poverty. The philosophy of the survival of the fittest does not soothe the class-conscious worker when he learns through his class literature that among the Italian pants-finishers of Chicago* the average weekly wage is $1.31, and the average number of weeks employed in the year is 27.85. Likewise when he reads:** "Every room in these reeking tenements houses a family or two. In one room a missionary found a man ill with small-pox, his wife just recovering from her confinement, and the children running about half naked and covered with dirt. Here are seven people living in one underground kitchen, and a little dead child lying in the same room. Here live a widow and her six children, two of whom are ill with scarlet fever. In another, nine brothers and sisters, from twenty-nine years of age downward, live, eat, and sleep together."

*From figures presented by Miss Nellie Mason Auten in the American Journal of Sociology, and copied extensively by the trade-union and Socialist press.

**"The Bitter Cry of Outcast London."

Wanted: A New Land of Development

And likewise, when he reads:* "When one man, fifty years old, who has worked all his life, is compelled to beg a little money to bury his dead baby, and another man, fifty years old, can give ten million dollars to enable his daughter to live in luxury and bolster up a decaying foreign aristocracy, do you see nothing amiss?"

And on the other hand, the class-conscious worker reads the statistics of the wealthy classes, knows what their incomes are, and how they get them. True, down all the past he has known his own material misery and the material comfort of the dominant classes, and often has this knowledge led him to intemperate acts and unwise rebellion. But today, and for the first time, because both society and he have evolved, he is beginning to see a possible way out. His ears are opening to the propaganda of Socialism, the passionate gospel of the dispossessed. But it docs not inculcate a turning back. The way through is the way out, he understands, and with this in mind he draws up the programme.

It is quite simple, this programme. Everything is moving in his direction, toward the day when he will take charge. The trust? Ah, no. Unlike the trembling middle-class man and the small capitalist, he sees nothing at which to be frightened. He likes the trust. He exults in the trust, for it is largely doing the task for him. It socializes production; this done, there remains nothing for him to do but socialize distribution, and all is accomplished. The trust? "It organizes industry on an enormous, labor-saving scale, and abolishes childish, wasteful competition." It is a gigantic object lesson, and it preaches his political economy far more potently than he can preach it. He points to the trust, laughing scornfully in the face of the orthodox economists. "You told me this thing could not be,"** he thunders. "Behold, the thing is!"

He sees competition in the realm of production passing away. When the captains of industry have thoroughly organized production, and got everything running smoothly, it will be very easy for him to eliminate the profits by stepping in and having the thing run for himself. And the captain of industry, if he be good, may be given the privilege of continuing the management on a fair salary. The sixty millions of dividends which the Standard Oil Company

---

*An item from the Social Democratic Herald. Hundreds of these items, culled from current happenings, are published weekly in the papers of the workers.

**Karl Marx, the great Socialist, worked out the trust development forty years ago, for which he was laughed at by the orthodox economists.

The War of the Classes

annually declares will be distributed among the workers. The same with the great United States Steel Corporation. The president of that corporation knows his business. Very good. Let him become Secretary of the Department of Iron and Steel of the United States. But, since the chief executive of a nation of seventy-odd millions works for $50,000 a year, the Secretary of the Department of Iron and Steel must expect to have his salary cut accordingly. And not only will the workers take to themselves the profits of national and municipal monopolies, but also the immense revenues which the dominant classes today draw from rents, and mines, and factories, and all manner of enterprises.

All this would seem very like a dream, even to the worker, if it were not for the fact that like things have been done before. He points triumphantly to the aristocrat of the eighteenth century, who fought, legislated, governed, and dominated society, but who was shorn of power and displaced by the rising bourgeoisie. Ay, the thing was done, he holds. And it shall be done again, but this time it is the proletariat who does the shearing. Sociology has taught him that m-i-g-h-t spells "right." Every society has been ruled by classes, and the classes have ruled by sheer strength, and have been overthrown by sheer strength. The bourgeoisie, because it was the stronger, dragged down the nobility of the sword; and the proletariat, because it is the strongest of all, can and will drag down the bourgeoisie.

And in that day, for better or worse, the common man becomes the master — for better, he believes. It is his intention to make the sum of human happiness far greater. No man shall work for a bare living wage, which is degradation. Every man shall have work to do, and shall be paid exceedingly well for doing it. There shall be no slum classes, no beggars. Nor shall there be hundreds of thousands of men and women condemned, for economic reasons, to lives of celibacy or sexual infertility. Every man shall be able to marry, to live in healthy, comfortable quarters, and to have all he wants to eat as many times a day as he wishes. There shall no longer be a life-and-death struggle for food and shelter. The old heartless law of development shall be annulled.

All of which is very good and very fine. And when these things have come to pass, what then? Of old, by virtue of their weakness and inefficiency in the struggle for food and shelter, the race was purged of its weak and inefficient members. But this will no longer obtain. Under the new order the weak and the progeny of the weak

Wanted: A New Land of Development

will have a chance for survival equal to that of the strong and the progeny of the strong. This being so, the premium upon strength will have been withdrawn, and on the face of it the average strength of each generation, instead of continuing to rise, will begin to decline.

When the common man's day shall have arrived, the new social institutions of that day will prevent the weeding out of weakness and inefficiency. All, the weak and the strong, will have an equal chance for procreation. And the progeny of all, of the weak as well as the strong, will have an equal chance for survival. This being so, and if no new effective law of development be put into operation, then progress must cease. And not only progress, for deterioration would at once set in. It is a pregnant problem. What will be the nature of this new and most necessary law of development? Can the common man pause long enough from his undermining labors to answer? Since he is bent upon dragging down the bourgeoisie and reconstructing society, can he so reconstruct that a premium, in some unguessed way or other, will still be laid upon the strong and efficient so that the human type will continue to develop? Can the common man, or the uncommon men who are allied with him, devise such a law? Or have they already devised one? And if so, what is it?

How I Became a Socialist

IT is quite fair to say that I became a Socialist in a fashion somewhat similar to the way in which the Teutonic pagans became
Christians — it was hammered into me. Not only was I not looking for Socialism at the time of my conversion, but I was fighting it.
I was very young and callow, did not know much of anything, and
though I had never even heard of a school called "Individualism," I
sang the paean of the strong with all my heart.

This was because I was strong myself. By strong I mean that I
had good health and hard muscles, both of which possessions are
easily accounted for. I had lived my childhood on California
ranches, my boyhood hustling newspapers on the streets of a
healthy Western city, and my youth on the ozone-laden waters of
San Francisco Bay and the Pacific Ocean. I loved life in the open,
and I toiled in the open, at the hardest kinds of work. Learning no
trade, but drifting along from job to job, I looked on the world and
called it good, every bit of it. Let me repeat, this optimism was
because I was healthy and strong, bothered with neither aches nor
weaknesses, never turned down by the boss because I did not look
fit, able always to get a job at shovelling coal, sailorizing, or manual
labor of some sort.

And because of all this, exulting in my young life, able to hold
my own at work or fight, I was a rampant individualist. It was very
natural. I was a winner. Wherefore I called the game, as I saw it
played, or thought I saw it played, a very proper game for *men*. To be
a *man* was to write man in large capitals on my heart. To adventure
like a man, and fight like a man, and do a man's work (even for a
boy's pay) — these were things that reached right in and gripped hold
of me as no other thing could. And I looked ahead into long vistas of
a hazy and interminable future, into which, playing what I conceived
to be *man's* game, I should continue to travel with unfailing health,
without accidents, and with muscles ever vigorous. As I say, this
future was interminable. I could see myself only raging through life
without end like one of Nietzsche's *blond=beasts,* lustfully roving
and conquering by sheer superiority and strength.

As for the unfortunates, the sick, and ailing, and old, and
maimed, I must confess I hardly thought of them at all, save that I
vaguely felt that they, barring accidents, could be as good as I if

80

How I Became a Socialist

they wanted to real hard, and could work just as well. Accidents? Well, they represented *fate,* also spelled out in capitals, and there was no getting around *fate.* Napoleon had had an accident at Waterloo, but that did not dampen my desire to be another and later Napoleon. Further, the optimism bred of a stomach which could digest scrap iron and a body which flourished on hardships did not permit me to consider accidents as even remotely related to my glorious personality.

I hope I have made it clear that I was proud to be one of Nature's strong-armed noblemen. The dignity of labor was to me the most impressive thing in the world. Without having read Carlyle, or Kipling, I formulated a gospel of work which put theirs in the shade. Work was everything. It was sanctification and salvation. The pride I took in a hard day's work well done would be inconceivable to you. It is almost inconceivable to me as I look back upon it. I was as faithful a wage slave as ever capitalist exploited. To shirk or malinger on the man who paid me my wages was a sin, first, against myself, and second, against him. I considered it a crime second only to treason and just about as bad.

In short, my joyous individualism was dominated by the orthodox bourgeois ethics. I read the bourgeois papers, listened to the bourgeois preachers, and shouted at the sonorous platitudes of the bourgeois politicians. And I doubt not, if other events had not changed my career, that I should have evolved into a professional strike-breaker, (one of President Eliot's American heroes), and had my head and my earning power irrevocably smashed by a club in the hands of some militant trades-unionist.

Just about this time, returning from a seven months' voyage before the mast, and just turned eighteen, I took it into my head to go tramping. On rods and blind baggages I fought my way from the open West where men bucked big and the job hunted the man, to the congested labor centres of the East, where men were small potatoes and hunted the job for all they were worth. And on this new *blond-beast* adventure I found myself looking upon life from a new and totally different angle. I had dropped down from the proletariat into what sociologists love to call the "submerged tenth," and I was startled to discover the way in which that submerged tenth was recruited.

I found there all sorts of men, many of whom had once been as good as myself and just as *blond-beast;* sailor-men, soldier-men, labor-men, all wrenched and distorted and twisted out of shape by

The War of the Classes

toil and hardship and accident, and cast adrift by their masters like so many old horses. I battered on the drag and slammed back gates with them, or shivered with them in box cars and city parks, listening the while to life-histories which began under auspices as fair as mine, with digestions and bodies equal to and better than mine, and which ended there before my eyes in the shambles at the bottom of the Social Pit.

And as I listened my brain began to work. The woman of the streets and the man of the gutter drew very close to me. I saw the picture of the Social Pit as vividly as though it were a concrete thing, and at the bottom of the Pit I saw them, myself above them, not far, and hanging on to the slippery wall by main strength and sweat. And I confess a terror seized me. What when my strength failed? when I should be unable to work shoulder to shoulder with the strong men who were as yet babes unborn? And there and then I swore a great oath. It ran something like this:

All my days I have worked hard with my body, and according to the number of days I have worked, by just that much am I neared the bottom of the pit. I shall climb out of the pit, but not by the muscles of my body shall I climb out. I shall do no more hard work, and may god strike me dead if I do another day's hard work with my body more than I absolutely have to do.

And I have been busy ever since running away from hard work. Incidentally, while tramping some ten thousand miles through the United States and Canada, I strayed into Niagara Falls, was nabbed by a fee-hunting constable, denied the right to plead guilty or not guilty, sentenced out of hand to thirty days' imprisonment for having no fixed abode and no visible means of support, handcuffed and chained to a bunch of men similarly circumstanced, carted down country to Buffalo, registered at the Erie County Penitentiary, had my head clipped and my budding mustache shaved, was dressed in convict stripes, compulsorily vaccinated by a medical student who practised on such as we, made to march the lock-step, and put to work under the eyes of guards armed with Winchester rifles —— all for adventuring in *blond-beastly* fashion. Concerning further details deponent sayeth not, though he may hint that some of his plethoric national patriotism simmered down and leaked out of the bottom of his soul somewhere —— at least, since that experience he finds that he cares more for men and women and little children than for imaginary geographical lines.

How I Became a Socialist

To return to my conversion. I think it is apparent that my rampant individualism was pretty effectively hammered out of me, and something else as effectively hammered in. But, just as I had been an individualist without knowing it, I was now a Socialist without knowing it, withal, an unscientific one. I had been reborn, but not renamed, and I was running around to find out what manner of thing I was. I ran back to California and opened the books. I do not remember which ones I opened first. It is an unimportant detail anyway. I was already It, whatever It was, and by aid of the books I discovered that It was a Socialist. Since that day I have opened many books, but no economic argument, no lucid demonstration of the logic and inevitableness of Socialism affects me as profoundly and convincingly as I was affected on the day when I first saw the walls of the Social Pit rise around me and felt myself slipping down, down, into the shambles at the bottom.